THE
EXPERTS
CURE

HOW ENTREPRENEURS ARE
CHANGING THE WORLD

THE
EXPERTS
CURE

HOW ENTREPRENEURS ARE
CHANGING THE WORLD

— Written by —

Rob Kosberg, Joanie Marx, Josh Coats, Cassady Cayne, Dr. Gena Lester,
Khaled Fattal, Kim Reutzel, Michael Chang, Marc & Krist Geriene,
Christopher Music, Dr. Gail L Clifford, MD, Peter Magana, Helena T. Jung,
Victor Allen, Jeff Rogers, Kelli Nguyen-Ha, Dr. Richard Kelley, Dr. Atousa Mahdavi,
Joyce Lacey, Christman & Molly Howard, Bashir Muhammad-Jordan

Published by Best Seller Publishing®, Pasadena, CA
Best Seller Publishing® is a registered trademark.
Printed in the United States of America.
ISBN: _____

For more information, please write:
Best Seller Publishing®
253 N. San Gabriel Blvd, Unit B
Pasadena, CA 91107
or call 1 (626) 765 9750

Visit us online at:
www.BestSellerPublishing.org

"YOUR **TEST** MAY HAVE COME BACK **NEGATIVE**, BUT HAVE YOU BEEN **STAYING POSITIVE**?"

— **BRENDA BOWERS,**

BEST-SELLING AUTHOR OF *WORLD CHANGERS AND DIFFERENCE MAKERS: A COMPREHENSIVE GUIDE TO TRANSFORM YOUR LIFE AND MEND THE WORLD ONE SPHERE AT A TIME*

TABLE OF CONTENTS

INTRODUCTION

I remember the first time I heard that there is a crater on the moon called the Kosberg crater. I was, to say the least, quite taken aback (and yeah, pretty excited!).

My dad told me that we had a relative (a distant one) from our family's ancestral home in Belarus. My great-great-grandparents came to the United States from Russia in the late 1890s through New York, to escape Jewish persecution, while many relatives stayed behind.

One of those relatives was Semyon Kosberg. He was quite literally a rocket scientist during World War II and became the number two man in the Russian space program. He went on to receive the Order of Lenin, the highest award given to a civilian by the former Soviet Union, as well as many other awards, and of course had a crater on the moon named after him.

His life became of interest to me when my middle son Jake began pursuing a career in science. Jake would eventually go on to receive his degree in advanced mathematics and currently works for NASA (crazy, right?!).

The unfortunate thing for me is that so little is actually known about Semyon Kosberg besides a Wikipedia page and random writings about the Russian space program. He and the top scientist both ended up dying within a few months of each other under mysterious circumstances.

As the founder of Best Seller Publishing (BSP), all I can think is: what if he had written a book? What if there were a memoir of his life and experiences?

As a *Wall Street Journal* best-selling author and founder of a company that has launched over 1,000 books, you can probably understand my frustration.

The important question is: will others wish they knew your story as well?

I believe you already know the answer to that question.

So many people are confused and perhaps even scared about getting started with their own books. Well, I think you'll be happy to know that I personally made every mistake imaginable with my first book, from paying a ghostwriter a huge amount of money and getting absolute garbage to believing some of the book-marketing experts out there and paying for one-off services, like press releases or email drops — all with zero results.

In the midst of your book-writing challenges (which you will absolutely face), you will have two options to choose from. It will be time to either decide what you really believe about writing your book and double down on your commitment or, quite frankly, give up the project all together.

Gary Keller of Keller Williams Realty International has something to say about this. The first book he wrote was called *The Millionaire Real Estate Agent: It's Not About the Money ... It's About Being the Best You Can Be!* He has gone on to write many other books since then. Recently I was reading one of his books, titled *The ONE Thing: The Surprisingly Simple Truth Behind Extraordinary Results.* On page 40 of his book, he relates how he came up with the idea to write a book. He says,

> "In 2001, I called a meeting of our key executive team. As fast as we were growing, we were still not acknowledged by the very top people in our industry. I challenged our group to brainstorm 100 ways to turn this situation around. It took us all day to come up with the list. The next morning, we narrowed the list down to ten ideas, and from there we chose just one big idea. The one that we decided on was that I would write a book on how to become an elite performer in our industry. It worked. Eight years later that one book had not only become a

national bestseller, but also had morphed into a series of books with total sales of over a million copies. In an industry of about a million people, one thing changed our image forever."[1]

Today, Keller Williams is the largest real estate brokerage in the world, and Gary Keller is a billionaire. Did it work for him? Was there magic in a book for him?

I also believed there was magic for me in a book.

I wrote my first book strictly for commercial reasons. I believed that there was magic in a book for me to help me grow a business, in a terrible economy in 2009, and help me grow my income and impact.

This magic isn't found just in the words that we put on the page and the expertise that we give our audience. The magic is found in how we're viewed because of the book. I call this idea "the hierarchy of desire." Simply put, the concept of the hierarchy of desire is that as your celebrity increases in the eyes of your ideal client, so too does your attractiveness. This leads to more and better clients.

The magic is in how your book propels you from generalist or even specialist to expert, and eventually thought leader and celebrity in your prospects' eyes.

And, as we like to say at BSP, you go from hunting for clients to becoming the hunted. Let me explain my big break, if I may.

After all the aforementioned mistakes and far too long in finishing, quite frankly, I finally had my book done, but wondered: now what? I didn't exactly know what to do, other than knowing that I needed to get my book into people's hands.

Mind you, this was all before podcasting, Facebook, Twitter, or any social media, for that matter. (It is so much easier for us to communicate our message today.)

So what did I do? I began sending my books to local radio stations and suggesting that they have me on their radio shows as a financial authority. After all, I was a best-selling author on the topic, and I could discuss the financial trauma and difficulties that many of their listeners were going through at the time.

1. Gary Keller and Jay Papasan, *The ONE Thing: The Surprisingly Simple Truth Behind Extraordinary Results* (Portland, OR: Bard Press, 2013), 40.

After sending my book, I would follow up with a telephone call to the local radio station manager. I kept following up until finally landing my first interview on a local station.

The interview was a standard four to five minutes, with the interviewer asking me questions and me presenting options for people financially. The interview went well, and at the end of that five-minute spot I offered anyone who was interested in learning more and getting help a free copy of my best-selling book. In fact, I would even pay the shipping — there was no charge whatsoever.

This was long before the idea of free-plus-shipping funnels that we see online now — which, by the way, work like gangbusters. I knew that if I could speak directly to people who had these challenges, I could present solutions for them and perhaps they would become clients of mine.

The radio interview was done live, and the station also played the recording several other times during the day. The very first night it aired, I was in my office by myself at about 6:00 p.m. when the phone rang.

I answered the phone and said, "This is Rob, how may I help you?"

The person on the other line simply said, "Is this Rob Kosberg?"

My first thought was, *Oh, man, I hope this isn't somebody I owe money to* (insert humor, kinda). This was shortly after the financial crisis in 2007–8 and the collapse of my real estate business. Another story for another day.

I said, "Yes, this is Rob, how can I help you?"

She said, "Wow, I can't believe I'm actually speaking to you. This is Rob Kosberg, the author and the person I heard on the radio, right?"

And I said, "Why, yes, yes it is."

At that moment, I personally experienced the magic of a book. I had never met this person, yet she had heard me on the radio, heard about my book, and because of that saw me as an authority and perhaps even as a celebrity. We spoke for about twenty minutes, and she became a client that night. No hardcore sales techniques were needed. No special closes. She needed help, and I was the authority who could help her.

I thought, *Maybe I'm onto something here?*

I started doing more radio interviews. I started spending a little bit of money on paid radio ads, and after about eight months, I even had my own radio show. Within a year, I was doing four hours of live radio every single week, offering my book for free (and shipped for free) to get it into people's hands.

We did over a million dollars in the first year — in a terrible economy — and then multimillions thereafter. It was all done by using my best-selling book.

Since that time, and completely organically (initially), people have been coming to me for help with their own books. At first, I didn't even know if I could help them, but now I have seen 1,000-plus authors tell their stories and make a difference in the world!

(For a free copy of my *Wall Street Journal* best-selling book, go to www.publishpromoteprofit.com.)

Whether you are looking to grow your authority and income by expressing your expertise in a book, or simply looking to tell your story for loved ones and future generations, your book is waiting to be written. It can be your gateway to greater authority, celebrity, and client attraction, as well as a source of joy to future generations and loved ones.

This book is titled *The Experts Cure: How Entrepreneurs are Changing the World*, and each expert is taking a chapter to tell their story. My hope is that you will gain inspiration from what you read and that you will, perhaps, begin to tell your own story as well.

ABOUT ROB KOSBERG

Rob Kosberg is a *Wall Street Journal* and *USA Today* best-selling author and the founder of Best Seller Publishing. He has been featured on ABC, NBC, CBS, and Fox, in *Forbes* and *Entrepreneur* magazines, as well as in hundreds of other shows, podcasts, magazines, and articles.

Rob's *Publish. Promote. Profit.* book and system have been used by tens of thousands of authors in dozens of countries. Simply put, Rob helps entrepreneurs become the go-to authority in their market by writing, launching, and profiting from a best-selling book.

CHAPTER 1:

THE INVISIBLE CUSTOMER WITH ALL THE MONEY®

BY JOANIE MARX

For as long as I could remember, I have been transforming nothing into something through the magic of storytelling.

At four years old, I took lemons off our tree in the backyard and made lemonade, calling it "Joan's Tasty Lemonade," which I sold from a table stand in our driveway.

At eight, I took our peaches and made peach pies that I sold to the neighbors.

At thirteen, I took alfalfa seeds, sprouted and packaged them, and then sold them to the local grocery and health food stores as "Joan's Alfalfa Sprouts — Nature's Most Perfect Food."

At twenty-six, I turned a ball of string and twenty dollars into a successful, multimillion-dollar consumer product company.

At forty, my yearning to be an actress could no longer be denied. I entered Hollywood at an age when most actresses were being told they were too old. Thirty years later, I still enjoy a successful career as an actress, producer, and spokeswoman for regional and national brands.

Just when I thought I had reached the peak of my career, something unexpected happened that changed everything. I became a Baby Boomer advocate, wrote two best-selling books, and was a sought-after consultant, advisor, and spokeswoman for brands who want to engage the 50+ market on an emotionally relevant level.

It all started at a luncheon with two of my longtime friends. There, I listened to my sorority sister's heartbreaking story. She sadly shared her dismay that due to her age, there were a lack of options for love, happiness, and fulfillment in her life. Mind you, this was coming from a bright, educated, and pretty woman.

I experienced gender discrimination early on in my entrepreneurial career and was exposed to age discrimination in Hollywood. Now I was seeing the lies and myths about love, happiness, and aging play out in the lives of dear friends. I could not stand by and accept this.

Leaving the luncheon that day, I was not clear on what I would do, but I knew three things for certain.

One, I had a gift for storytelling and knew how to harness its power to magically transform nothing into something. Two, I needed to better understand what I was up against, which required lots of research. And three, I vowed to do battle against these myths and stereotypes about aging that so deeply affected my friends.

To my shock and horror, I came to realize the sheer magnitude of damage these myths and stereotypes have wrought on society. They are not just a daily reality for people in the 50-and-over club. Tens of millions of people in younger generations are beset by them as well, particularly women.

UNSEXY, UNPROFITABLE, AND OBSOLETE

You see them everywhere you look. Often referred to as Baby Boomers and Generation X, those in the 50-and-over club, or fast approaching it, make up over 103 million people in the United States. They are "The Invisible Customer with All the Money®."

Despite being a part of the exclusive, lucrative, and ever-growing 50-and-over club, this critically important part of society is deeply misunderstood and surprisingly ignored. So how did they go from once being the most coveted consumer in the world when they were young to now being The Invisible Customer with All the Money®?

The answer is the media's reliance on outdated myths and false narratives that paint an unflattering picture of the 50+ market as unsexy, unprofitable, and thus obsolete. This distorted perception can be rewritten, and thankfully, it already is. To ensure it continues to change, your presence, support, and creative talents are needed.

Whether you are personally in the 50-and-over club or raised by someone who is, the quality of your life and your career success depend on this audience being seen, heard, felt, and valued more than you may realize. If that seems like a bold declaration now, it won't be when we finish our journey together through this chapter.

Storytelling Magician™

If you represent a brand whose product or service relies on the financial affluence and social influence of The Invisible Customer with All the Money®, your firm's profits greatly depend on crafting engaging campaigns. The storylines for these campaigns must be emotionally relevant and authentically aligned with the reality of the 50+ consumer, not on outdated myths and dismissive stereotypes.

This is where I come in, as a Storytelling Magician™.

Contrary to what many believe, profiting off The Invisible Customer with All the Money® requires a lot more than giving loyalty discounts or analyzing data on spending habits. If entrepreneurs and business leaders genuinely desire to change the world for the better, it does not start by making more money. It begins by taking responsibility for the stories we tell and rewriting the ones we once thought were unchangeable.

Albert Einstein spoke to this when he famously said, "We cannot solve our problems with the same level of thinking we used when we created them."

As a Storytelling Magician™, rather than pulling a rabbit out of a tall black hat, I am waving my magic wand, which produces a key to unlock previously closed doors to the growth of your brand. The Invisible Customer with all the Money® is that magic key.

Once you know how to use this key and which doors it opens, you will discover new, lucrative opportunities that were once unseen. But how and where do these distorted perceptions and blind spots with the 50+ consumer show up in actual campaigns? I will share one I was personally involved in.

CAN YOU "BE MORE FEEBLE"?

The direction was clear, and yet I was unmistakably confused. I glanced quizzically at the director. He nodded at me, not so much picking up on my confusion but more to let me know it was time for me to "be more feeble."

This scene was for a national commercial highlighting a new offer from a leading telecommunications brand. Having beaten out a hundred-plus talented actors to get this far, this was a final audition that was going to come down to me and ten other gifted women in the same age range.

Following the director's suggestion, I proceeded to quickly interpret what being "more feeble" meant in the context of the scene itself. It called for me to be a sixty-five-year-old grandmother driving my young grandson to a well-known mobile store where we would be taking advantage of a new, less-expensive family plan that involved three new smartphones.

An actor's talent is in their choices. In this instance, the choice was simple: embody a feeble old woman driving her grandson to a mobile store. This is precisely what I did. My young costar, who was fifteen, and I finished our second take flawlessly. We smiled at each other and congratulated ourselves.

Exiting the makeshift car, the director quickly came up to me and excitedly exclaimed, "Great job, Joanie. That was absolutely perfect!" After thanking the director and ad agency representative, I grabbed my belongings and was leaving the studio when the casting director came up to me.

We have a long-standing relationship, as she has helped me get booked for other commercials over the years. She said, "Joanie, you really are a magician at improvisation. Awesome job on adjusting to changes in the script."

I thanked her and then asked if she had any insights on how being "more feeble" became the focus of the commercial, since it was not part of the original audition. She took a moment to consider her answer and then said bluntly, "The ad agency changed it at the last minute. They're paying the bill and calling the shots."

DOES YOUTH REALLY EQUAL MORE PROFITS?

The casting director is right: the one with the money calls the shots. But what about the consumer with all the money? Why are billions of dollars and vast amounts of human resources continuously focused on a youthful consumer who is not nearly as affluent or as influential over household spending habits as The Invisible Customer with All the Money®?

Baby Boomers and Generation X spend over $900 billion annually, and this staggering number is on the rise. It underscores what has been confirmed by recent Nielsen studies in terms of generational spending. They reported that "Between now and 2030, the 18–49 segment is expected to grow +12%, while the 50+ segment will expand by +34%."[2]

The 50-and-over club are also big spenders and avid users of technology. This was illustrated by Pew Research, who stated that "there has been significant growth in tech adoption since 2012 among older generations — particularly Gen Xers and Baby Boomers."[3] Yet when it comes to advertising campaigns geared toward technology, particularly online ads, only a meager five percent focus on the 50+ market or visually showcase them.

Then there is "The Great Wealth Transfer." According to a Harvard University study, in the next decade, more than 27.7 million Generation X consumers will be a part of the 50-and-over club. More than just being tech- and media-savvy consumers, this so-called "forgotten generation" will directly benefit from the $68 trillion that will be passed down from Boomers to their immediate heirs between 2020 and 2061.

2. Vaughan Emsley, "Don't Underestimate the Market Power of the 50+ Crowd," *Harvard Business Review,* January 9, 2020, https://hbr.org/2020/01/dont-underestimate-the-market-power-of-the-50-crowd.

3. Emily A. Vogels, "Millennials stand out for their technology use, but older generations also embrace digital life," *Fact Tank: News in The Numbers* (blog), *Pew Research Center,* September 9, 2019, https://www.pewresearch.org/fact-tank/2019/09/09/us-generations-technology-use/.

Despite overwhelming evidence to the contrary, the myth that people over the age of fifty are technology-challenged, slow, feeble, unsexy, and obsolete remains entrenched in the perceptions of those creating the narrative for online and offline campaigns. This perception is not even close to being accurate for today's 50-and-over population and can no longer be relied upon to grow and sustain long-term profits.

WHO DO THEY THINK WE ARE?

After speaking with the casting director, I walked outside the studio, where I ran into some of the other female actors who had auditioned just before me. All of us audition for the same roles, which are described as "older woman over fifty." Most of those auditions come with a specific request to wear a white-haired wig.

One of them asked, "So, how did it go, Joanie?"

I could not wait to take off my little old lady wig. With it stuffed back into my purse, I answered, "They asked me to be more feeble."

All the women looked at one another and one spoke up first: "Me too." Another chimed in, "Why is it assumed that a sixty-five-year-old woman is feeble? Who do they think we are in real life?" One answered, "Honey, this is the land of make-believe. It ain't real life."

A fourth woman then asked the one question we all knew the answer to. "If this commercial was supposed to reflect real life, what does being more feeble have to do with buying a smartphone for her grandson?"

"Absolutely nothing," I said.

Once inside my car, I took a moment to reflect on this experience. I began to clearly see the correlation between the lunch with my sorority sister the year before and this audition. A mix of anger and inspiration rose up in me.

Without a clue as to where my justified rage would take me, or what this wave of inspiration would lead to, I knew it was now or never. I needed to reveal how companies can achieve more success and how individuals can experience greater fulfillment by rewriting the false storylines about love, aging, and happiness.

If not me, who? And if not right now, when?

THIS IS WHO I AM

Determined to change how the world views love, aging, and happiness, over the next ten years I summoned my magic for storytelling and created something out of nothing.

I wrote, produced, and starred in "The McGranny Secret™," a three-part McDonald's spec commercial with my newly registered slogans "Drive Thru & Make It Your Own®" and "The Invisible Customer with All the Money®." This was followed by a series of national and regional radio interviews, podcasts, articles, and online campaigns, which led me to writing two best-selling books.

At sixty-nine, I wrote my first book, *Facelifts, Money & Prince Charming: Break Baby Boomer Myths & Live Your Best Life*. It became a #1 Amazon Best Seller. At seventy-four, I wrote my second book, *In Spite Of...: How to Refocus & Renew Your Life® In Spite of the Obstacles on the Path to Love & Happiness*, which became a #1 International Amazon Best Seller.

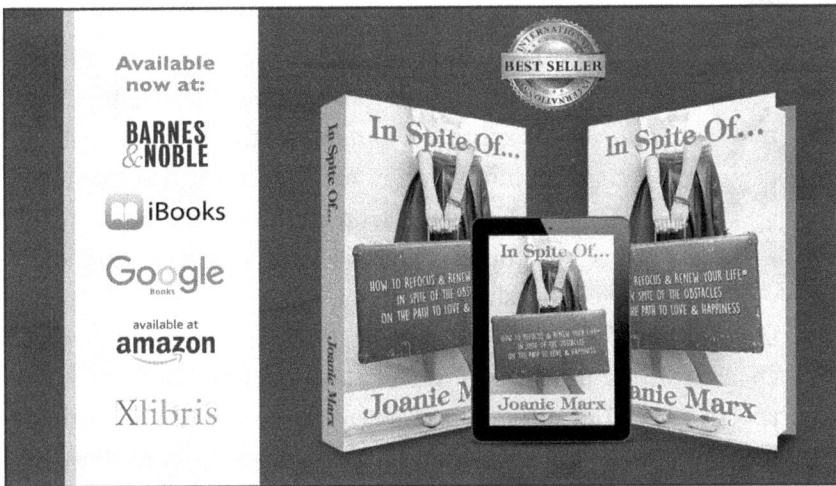

This journey has taken me to places within myself I did not know existed, healing many unhealed childhood traumas. It also led to incredible business opportunities and creative collaborations with amazing people who have both changed and enlightened my life. Through the magic of storytelling, the books, commercials, and campaigns I have created and been involved in have reached millions of people. But I am far from finished.

Today, I am more passionate than ever to show companies and all generations that doors of opportunity can be opened at any time and at any age when you Refocus & Renew Your Life®. And there has never been a more important time for doing so.

I have been many things in my career. In all I do to serve the vision of those I collaborate with, I am one thing above all else. I am a Storytelling Magician™. This is who I am. Creating value for the brands I represent, while making the world a better place, is what I do.

☆ ☆ ☆ ☆ ☆

ABOUT JOANIE MARX

An entrepreneurial trailblazer and brand spokeswoman, Joanie Marx is a two-time best-selling author who is known as a Storytelling Magician™.

Serving as an advisor, consultant, and brand spokeswoman, Joanie flips the script on outdated storylines, revealing not only how to connect with The Invisible Customer with all the Money* but how to build a lucrative and long-term relationship with them.

As a master storyteller with a proven track record in Hollywood as an actress, producer, and writer, Joanie brings a fresh new perspective on crafting genuine, engaging conversations with a multi-generational audience. She is a graduate of the University of California, Berkeley, with a degree in psychology.

Contact Joanie at joanie@joaniemarx.com.

To buy one of her books, visit Joanie's author page at Amazon.

Discover interview topics and book Joanie for your show at joaniemarx.com/interviewjoaniemarx.

Is your brand 50+ proof? Hire Joanie as your next consultant, advisor, and brand spokeswoman at joaniemarx.com.

CHAPTER 2:

THE MESS BEFORE SUCCESS

BY JOSH COATS

I'll never forget that moment. I was celebrating my third child being born. We had sent Paxton to the nursery to be taken care of after a long day in the hospital. About one hour later, we got a call.

"I'm sorry to inform you, but your son will not be able to return to the hospital room. We're going to have to keep him overnight for some additional tests," the nurse explained.

That's the last thing in the world any parent wants to hear. No explanation. No details. We were left to worry all night about what could be wrong with our son.

The next day, we had doctor after doctor stop by our room to try to explain to us what was wrong with our precious child. While I didn't really understand any of the explanations, I would later understand that our son was born with multiple deformities in his heart and would need at least one surgery to try to fix them.

We stayed in the hospital for six weeks, waiting for the first of what would turn into three different surgeries over a span of two and a half years.

As if that weren't hard enough, I was in the wrong career to have a child who would end up having several long stays in the hospital. I had spent the last six years detailing cars for a living. While it paid decent money, it was just enough to keep up with the bills. It was almost never enough to have any extra money, and we would usually spend October through December waiting for that magical tax return in January to save our lives and catch us up on the bills that we had fallen behind on.

For two and a half years I would feel myself constantly pulled in so many directions. I spent the night with my son most nights in the hospital, and then would go to work on almost no sleep at all. I would work as hard as I could for four or five hours and then go home to get a few hours of sleep before returning to the hospital at night.

Thankfully, my son would eventually come away from these surgeries a happy and healthy boy, who is turning ten this month as I write! But this critical season forced me to face a few realities about my life that I had previously ignored.

FEELING FAILURE

I realized that a life that does not give me the freedom to take care of my family isn't a life worth building. I also realized that while I was working my butt off to pay the bills and try to find time for my family, someone else was keeping the majority of the profits from my labor, all while playing golf and taking their family on vacations.

There had to be a way that I could do something I was passionate about, something I truly loved. And in doing so, surely there was a way to create a lifestyle that would reward my family instead of punishing them.

I didn't even know where to start. All I knew was that my older brother, who was a youth pastor, seemed to always be learning and growing. Every time we met up, he was telling me something he had learned from the most recent book he had read. I wasn't sure I could make time to read books, but I did have eight hours per day while I detailed cars. Maybe I could download podcasts and start to learn something new that way?

I pulled out my iPhone and subscribed to anything and everything that sounded interesting — everything from health to finance to business. As I listened to episode after episode, something in me awakened. I wasn't even sure what to do with all of this new information I was learning, but my soul felt on fire!

I later found someone by the name of John Maxwell on one of the podcasts I was listening to regularly. He seemed to be doing everything that I was starting to imagine myself doing, but was decades ahead of me. He had a certification program where you could be trained to be a speaker, coach, and trainer. I wasn't sure I knew what all of those things meant, but everything in me said I needed to jump.

A month later, I took my tax return and signed up. With the number one leadership trainer in the world on my side, surely I couldn't fail, right?

Wrong.

My first year, I drove all over Tulsa, Oklahoma, buying people coffee, putting on events, and trying everything I could to land clients who wanted to be coached by me. One year of listening to six to seven hours' worth of training per day, talking to everyone I knew, and following every game plan given to me. And all I was able to do was make $500.

I felt like a failure. I felt like maybe I wasn't cut out for this. I felt like maybe some people were special and I just wasn't one of them.

But my heart screamed for me to keep going. I reminded myself of the life I wanted to create for my kids. Most importantly, I told myself over and over and over that I'd rather tell my kids I tried and failed than tell them I gave up because I was too scared. So I persisted.

In year two, I took my business to social media, where I could meet more people in less time. I got a few breaks. I asked for referrals. And I slowly built up enough momentum to shift into another gear. My confidence was growing so fast that nothing could stop me. My fears were fading out and my faith was turning up louder than ever before.

PRINCIPLES OF SUCCESS

Fast-forward to the end of my second year, and I was able to walk away from my full-time job. I made my first $10K month, and everything I wanted to create for my family became a reality.

I went on to do $400K in my first full year of coaching full-time. I started this business at the age of thirty with hopes that I could somehow find a way to accomplish my dreams by the age of thirty-five. And here I am, about to turn thirty-seven, and I have built a multimillion-dollar business, am a best-selling author of the book *F*** Leadership*, and have a top 100 podcast (*Your PUSH Coach*).

What does this story have to do with you? What does it have to do with building a business during a global pandemic or hard times? Everything!

I've had the honor of coaching, mentoring, and interviewing dozens of six-, seven-, and even eight-figure earners over the last six years. When you break down their success, whether in a good economy or a bad economy, every success story comes down to the exact same principles as the story you just heard from me.

And anytime I go through a hard time in my life, whether it be my son's open-heart surgeries, or when I later went through a divorce and almost lost everything, or when the global pandemic happened, I always go back to these simple principles. These principles are how I originally built success, but also how I've built on that success, and how I've rebuilt success any time I've gone through a hard time.

Principle 1: Everything Starts with Personal Growth

I've said since my very first presentation that outward success is an expression of our inward growth. Our first reaction as humans is to look outside for a solution. We look at people with a lot of money and we go look at their Instagram and Twitter. We see their houses, money, and cars and think that if we just had what they have, we would be successful.

I always tell my clients to stop looking at the outward results that others get and instead study their daily habits. The things they do on a daily basis are how they got all of the houses and cars, not the other way around. I understand that this isn't a new concept, and you've probably read that personal growth is important in a hundred books. But in training thousands of people, I will tell you it's still the thing that gets overlooked the most. It's still the thing people avoid first and trust last.

Your mindset is the engine that drives the entire car of your business. And you can spend all day and night adding spoilers and rims, but if the engine is a piece of crap that needs to be restored, you won't be going anywhere.

Principle 2: Add Value Before You Ask for Value

I can remember walking into coffee shops and seeing business cards lying around for "free consultations" from life coaches and others who offered personal services. I can remember how icky they made me feel to think that I would meet up with someone just to be sold to.

I decided to do something completely different. Instead of offering free "consultations," I would just offer a free call. I sent around ten messages per day to people, offering them one free call to see if there was anything I could do to help them. This gave people something free and tangible and then allowed them to decide if it was worth paying for.

When the global pandemic happened, I decided that in harder times people needed that much more value and proof before they would purchase something. So I put together a Summit of Hope and gathered the most successful entrepreneurs I had contact with. We offered eighteen different speakers over the course of a week for the cost of a five-dollar donation to charity.

For an entire week, I just added value, encouraged people, and showed them how the top performers handled diversity in their business. I followed up the event with a massive free workshop where I ended up having one of my most successful sales weekends. If you want to get value, you have to give it first. And if you realize you need more value, you just have to turn up the amount you're willing to give!

Please be very careful to not be in a rush to make a sale. Instead, be in a rush to plant a seed. But remember that harvesting always takes time. It takes watering and nurturing.

Principle 3: Keep Marketing This Simple: Expand + Engage + Convert

I've watched a lot of people and businesses really thrive at one or two of these things, but the reason most businesses never take off is because they fail to do all three consistently and coherently.

I grew up in small churches where pastors constantly questioned why their church didn't grow more. They had great messages, a great mission, and even had a lot of great people. But they failed to realize just how many new people they would need to find to make up for the people that would decide to leave for one reason or another. I watched pastors take it so personally when people left. And often it would become a toxic environment, as they would then shift the culture to try to "keep" people instead of trying to grow.

My advice to you is to put just as much energy and attention into bringing in new people as you do into taking care of current people. You should treat every single person like they will be there forever, but be smart enough to know they probably won't be. You can do this organically through things like messaging people on social media (my preference) and meeting people in person, or you can do things like paid advertising. I highly recommend making sure your paid advertising is on a platform that can measure and track success, such as social media or Google.

Principle 4: Find Someone Who Has Already Done It

I partnered up with John Maxwell because I knew he was the greatest leadership talent in the world. But from there, I needed to learn new lessons. When I found Grant Cardone, I realized that he had the magic for motivation and goal achievement. So I listened to his books over and over and over. When I wanted to reach more people in less time, I invested in learning Facebook ads, which ended up being one of the main pillars of traffic and revenue for my business and is one of the main ways I keep scaling my business each year!

Every new season I ask myself: what do I need to learn next and who is the best in the world to learn it from? I am a constant student of personal growth, leadership, performance, and marketing. I believe that to be a successful entrepreneur, you'll need to be a constant student as well. The beautiful thing about being a student is that you become pandemic-proof. When the rest of the world is worried, in doubt, and in fear, you commit to learning how to navigate it. You commit to learning how to grow through it. And as a result, you are able to help others to do the same. And *that* is the most important part: giving back to others.

If you're someone who needs an expert in your life, I'd love to help. I know that social media and the Internet has made it easier than ever to find people, but harder than ever to connect with people. There are five million gurus and experts on any and every topic you could imagine, but very few people who actually know what they're talking about. I hope this book gives you access to several people, but if my story specifically speaks to you, I'd love to give you access to my Summit of Hope, a collection of interviews with eighteen speakers on how to build your business during a rough season in life. The only thing I ask for is a donation of $5 or more toward the International Network of Hearts. If you'd like to help rescue women and children from sex trafficking and get a ton of resources on how to build your business, you can go to www.joshcoats.com/summitofhope to get access!

You can find additional training resources and get a free copy of my book *F*** Leadership* at www.joshcoats.com.

Cheers to going all in on your dreams and changing the world!

ABOUT JOSH COATS

Josh Coats is a high-energy, no-excuses, no-BS motivational speaker and business coach. He is the #1 best-selling author of *F*** Leadership* and host of the top 100 podcast *Your PUSH Coach*, a podcast that takes you behind the curtain for 1:1 coaching sessions to help you to identify and overcome your limiting beliefs.

He has grown a 1:1 waiting list of over 100, trains thousands per month in online training groups, and travels the country to speak for events and retreats. His mission is to PUSH entrepreneurs to reach their full potential.

Josh lives in Tulsa, Oklahoma, with his fiancée Jenny Fuller and his kids Dakotah, Kaiden, Paxton, and Amaiah.

CHAPTER 3:

CHANGING OUR LIVES, FROM THE INSIDE OUT

By Cassady Cayne

IDENTITY, THE CONSTRUCTED SELF: HOW TO ASK OURSELVES THE RIGHT QUESTIONS TO UNLOCK A BRIGHTER FUTURE

In my work with clients and readers, darkness is never a stranger. Every day over the last five years, I've come face to face with people who have been through trauma and feel they can never truly be happy again. People who have lost hope and feel nothing will ever get better. Who, deep down, worry that maybe they're just not made for happiness, fulfillment, or a good life...

That was my experience too, so many times earlier in life. Growing up in a dysfunctional family setting with a clinically depressed father, I was shown by example that it was "normal" to suffer. That life was nothing but fleeting moments of light packed in struggle.

It's probably why I became so tenacious in my search for answers after my awakening, which happened after I lost my job in the media during the last recession and was forced to move back in with my parents due to a chronic health issue. As I had physical challenges and no job prospects due to the recession, I essentially had no option but to go within.

As I began exploring the unconscious, along with the mindsets, beliefs, and what makes up our identity and our life path, slowly but surely, it was like someone switched on the light in a long-shadowed room.

Bit by bit, I began experiencing the positive shifts that happen once we begin to look within, question our beliefs and habits, and unlock our perspective. When we stop running from our pain and face it, to start to heal.

Switching On the Light

The biggest thrill I experience in my work is when I hear from people a few months down the line. When I've guided them through shifting their mindset and healing old wounds, and they get back in touch to tell me how much has changed.

They feel like different people. They seem more alive, more present than before. Most of all, hope has been reignited in them. They see themselves and the world differently. They feel like a burden has been released and they feel free to embrace the future in light and wonder again. Often, they've returned to a childlike state of amazement they'd forgotten existed.

The beautiful thing is that these shifts are quite simple to trigger. It's within reach for all of us. But it's so deeply buried, most of us never think to try. We've been told there's no point. And because that point of view is so common, no one questions it.

Every single one of us is born innocent. But as we grow up, we're shown and told more and more about what being a human being is "supposed" to look like. Well-meaning people around us tell us who we are and what we can and can't do, and most of us inherit a pre-made "recipe" of identity from our family and social culture.

Nearly all of these assessments, statements, and identity markers come from the outside in. People know our name, where we come from, our social status ... but not what makes our heart sing with joy. People are told about our income level and our job title and family relations, but we rarely openly share the innermost things that make us who we are on an inner essential level.

Most often, the identity we live with isn't true to who we really are inside.

THE BAGGAGE WE TAKE ON

Bit by bit in life, we put up more and more walls around our movement and choice. We're painted into a corner and most of us don't think to walk away. Our father didn't lavish praise on us, so we begin to not take chances on jobs or dates because we've learned to expect rejection. Or all A grades were expected in childhood, so now we work sixty-hour weeks and rarely take time off because we're a go-getter.

There are endless varieties and examples of this, but in essence, so much of our life path is shaped by the identity we've built up or has been pushed onto us along the way. So many of us end up living a life essentially mapped out by someone else — family, hometown culture, peers, society… Through childhood experiences, wounds, and unconscious fears and shadows, we begin to hold ourselves back from living life fully.

So many of life's choices are made on automatic because of this "constructed" identity and the past wounds involved in it.

Identity and life path shifting in the new era.
Copyright: Adobe Stock

A New Era Where Life Is Not "Set in Stone"

I've both experienced this and been blessed to work through healing so much of the restriction I carried around for decades of my life — and now I get to guide others through the same.

When I began studying psychology, then later energy work and emotional healing, things began to click. I began to realize that who we are is not "set in stone" the way it's most often presented in life.

Who we are, and what we do with that, is so much more malleable and open to choice than most of us are ever told. The unfortunate thing is that often, *we* are the ones keeping ourselves locked up with restrictions… Why? Mostly due to fear. Fear that something bad will happen if we go beyond. Fear that love and acceptance will be taken away from us if we don't conform to others' ideas of who we are or should be.

It's not surprising considering that we're mammals, herd animals. Our brains are wired to keep us safe, and human biology has hardly changed since the Stone Age, according to science. Deep down, we tend to fear anything that may risk group protection, which our ancestors depended on for survival.

But now, in the 21st century, it often holds us hostage in a world full of more life-changing opportunity and expansion than ever before.

We're on the cusp of change as the flexibility of our life path becomes more and more widespread. In ages past, we may have been locked into one identity for life, but today, we and our self-perception and circumstances are evolving along with the fast shifts happening in society and online.

How We Often Stop Ourselves

In my work, I see so many people blossom after their self-perception changes. When they're shown how capable they are and how malleable their situation actually is, their view of themselves and life changes. After they face fears and heal old hurts, they begin to experience things differently. They feel like they get to start over after releasing the baggage of judgments and identity that they took on in their upbringing.

My role is to guide them to realize that first of all, there really is more for them in life than what they've been taught. To dismantle old blocks and "false limitations" they have accepted into their lives. Because again, although life can be challenging, many of the most lasting issues we have is that we stop ourselves, without even realizing it most of the time.

Like a house that started out brand-new and clean, we've put on so many layers of paint over and over that the shape has become distorted and unrecognizable. Once we start peeling off the layers, the judgments, we become freer.

Hope returns; we begin to see possibilities where we used to see only potential failure. We begin to feel loved by life again, instead of pitted against existence in the "human struggle."

I hear from people every single week who are stunned that something like this is possible, because they got so used to the belief that the old way was set in stone. That there was no choice. They thought they "just had to play the cards they had been dealt." And once they realize they're actually a lot freer than they believed, everything changes.

I've had people from all walks of life go through this process: Dylan from the UK who multiplied his income ten times over after realizing he'd put limits on himself, then took action to move beyond the old paradigm; Kali from the United States, who met her soulmate after releasing old heartbreak and opening up to love again; couples who got married after "working through their muck" and finding a deeper sense of harmony and shared unity.

So many clients and readers reporting that they truly feel love for themselves for the first time, finding a sense of deeper meaning.

When I hear that someone is seeing themselves and life differently, I know things are about to change for them because when our perspective changes, everything in our lives begins to shift as a result: our choices, our dynamics and relationships with other people, our work, our creativity, even our bodies.

When we go within and "recalibrate," when we heal and face the old shadows and wounds, it powerfully impacts the future. We begin to change our lives from the "inside out." Life begins to feel easier, more welcoming. We begin to feel that we are here for a reason, more loved by others, by life, and by ourselves.

WHAT DIFFERENTIATES TWO NEARLY IDENTICAL PEOPLE'S VERY DIFFERENT PATHS?

I've often asked myself: what was the difference between myself and my relatives of the same age, who had the same genetics as me, the same upbringing, the same socioeconomic background, and the same hometown with the same ethnicity, religion, and education?

What made me end up going for my dreams, helping others, expanding into reaching over a million readers and moving halfway across the world to live a life of passion, when they chose to stay in the safe limitations of our shared hometown?

Looking at all the factors, a key ingredient is identity. I saw myself differently as a result of reading and exploration of culture and historical figures who had nothing to do with where I came from, my gender, name, or family background. Through "invisible mentors," I was able to see differently. So although the "raw ingredients" matched between my relatives and I, how I saw that essence, differed.

I accessed a whole world of possibility via books and teachers and, as a result, saw myself as capable of more, where they chose to follow in the family footsteps. I saw the world as one of opportunity and adventure, where they mostly held back due to fear of the unknown. And that's not to say I didn't feel doubt or trepidation along the way — but I learned to keep going anyway. Again, a choice made from identity and worldview.

WHY IT'S NEVER TOO LATE

I love to share this, because my own journey is an example of how we don't need to be special or have advantages in life in order to achieve our dreams and change our circumstances. Do privilege and circumstances help? Of course.

But can we make something big happen anyway? Absolutely. There are countless stories of star athletes and famous actors who've overcome struggles and poverty to reach the top, CEOs and successful thought leaders who didn't make it through high school.

The world is full of inspiration. It's never too late. And above all, it's about how we see ourselves. The first step is to question what we've been taught about who we are and what's possible for us. Because inside, beneath all the "layers of paint" and judgments, you're a soul. You are you — who you would be if all those outer things faded away.

THE "EASY WAY" TO GET MORE OF WHAT WE WANT

We all want more joy, ease, and love in our lives. To feel like things run more smoothly, that life is a joy rather than a struggle. But positive change often feels hard to create. "Up-leveling" our identity is a simple yet massively powerful way to shift our lives for the better.

We don't have to wait for some huge outer factor to make positive change in our world. When we shift our identity, it "happens by itself." As our inner state changes, the outside begins to shift as well — without struggle. How? Identity drives our thoughts, emotions, habits, choices, and our behavior in every moment. It powerfully affects our relationships, our level of income, our career, and our life path.

It impacts our mental and emotional health, whether we're a great friend/parent/citizen or bring damage to ourselves and others. Identity can hold us back or fuel us to reach massive heights. It's the missing piece of the puzzle so many are looking for.

One major shift that's available to you and me and everyone right now is to know that the limits we've accepted as "real" are often not. To know that the future is so much more open to our positive input than we tend to think. We really are powerful once we open up to this possibility.

THE TRANSFORMATIVE POWER OF CHALLENGES

This last year, so many of us have faced more trials than we would ever have expected. But from my work with clients and readers all over the world, I know that no matter how hard things get, challenges also have the power to transform us and our lives for the better in the long term. Because challenge brings transformation, it makes us question the status quo in our lives. Once this storm passes, we'll be different.

Many of us awaken to a higher state of being through hardship that breaks us open into a new state. It may seem like we are facing darkness at this time, but in that darkness, the seeds of future growth are sown. As our "new normal" begins, we are new people. And we get to choose how that looks, who we are in this, more than most of us ever believed possible.

Learn more about Cassady Cayne and her transformational coaching work at www.cassadycayne.com.

ABOUT CASSADY CAYNE

Cassady Cayne is a best-selling author and personal growth coach focused on spiritual wellness and lifelong learning. Her work focuses on empowering people to unlock their true potential and thrive in their uniqueness.

With an academic background in psychology and history, Cassady grew up in a working-class family in northern Europe, raised with the belief that there was no higher power, existence was hard, and there was no deeper purpose to life. After losing her job in the last recession and struggling with depression, she experienced an unexpected spiritual awakening which completely changed her life path.

Since launching her blog four short years ago, Cassady's energy work and inspirational writing have gone on to reach over a million readers and clients worldwide. She has been featured in major media including *Psychology Today, Entrepreneur,* Yahoo Finance and more, speaking at the "You Can Heal Your Life Summit" alongside leading authors such as Dr. Deepak Chopra, Gabrielle Bernstein, and Dr. Joe Dispenza.

CHAPTER 4:

THE CROSSROADS
(TAKE A CHANCE ON DISCOVERING WHAT
MAKES YOU U-NIQUELY-U˙)

BY DR. GENA LESTER

I can say without a doubt that I was destined to be an entrepreneur. In third grade, I invited and brought twenty-seven kids to a church event and won a contest. In fifth grade, I collected the most Goodwill bags in Campfire Girls. I started a babysitting business in eighth grade, was booked solid every weekend, and stashed hundreds of dollars away in my sock drawer. I sold candy bars to pay for my drill team uniform and even sold pet rocks in my driveway. In my early twenties, I became a Tupperware distributor. I was consistently ranked number one in the nation in both sales and recruits. At twenty-nine, I partnered with a local church and started a private school that I ran for fourteen years. But none of this prepared me for my next entrepreneurial journey: at thirty-five, my husband was diagnosed with Parkinson's and my life was turned upside down.

While running the private school I started, I went on my own educational journey, completing a double master's, a PhD, and a doctorate degree over a six-year span. As my husband's condition deteriorated, I knew that he was in need of full-time care. With the loss of his income and mounting medical bills, I had to make a choice between caring for him and working an outside job. I was confident that I could start my own business, one that would allow me to be at home with him while providing for our family — after all, I had a history of starting and running successful businesses. The difference this time was that it was all up to me. I did not have the safety net of my husband's job or a low-cost start-up; this time, we were living on disability, which barely paid our bills.

A PASSION FOR DISCOVERY

I am a lifelong learner and know the value of a college degree. I come from a long line of college graduates, including my grandmother, who went to college at a time when most women did not. I had already walked two of my kids successfully through the college process. Their success had brought families knocking on my door, asking if I could help them. Thus, my next journey began. That was the easy part — the hard part was figuring out how to grow my business with zero money. My youngest was a junior in high school and was starting her college journey, so I knew that I had access to other high school parents.

I put an offer together and began calling friends and offering my services. The first year included three students, all of whom were accepted to their perfect college with scholarships totaling over a million dollars. Year two included my daughter and five other students. This group received over four million dollars in scholarships. My daughter walked away with three full rides and was able to choose where she wanted to go to college. I will always cherish the early days of meeting students at my dining room table, which led to my now six-figure business that is fully online. Even though my husband passed away, the journey provided me with a business that I love and a freedom that before I had only dreamed of.

When you consider that life is short and that we spend over half of it working, it is important that we choose a career we love. I am excited to get up each morning and help others step into their future, one that they are excited about. Most college admissions consultants typically focus on students looking for Ivy League schools — and yes, I have had students accepted to the Ivy League and top-ranked schools. But it is about more than an Ivy League education. My background in both business and education allows me to help teens find their passion and connect to it in their college journey.

For those who applied to college fifteen-plus years ago, applying and getting in was a much easier process. You applied to three or four colleges at the most. It was rare to apply as an out-of-state applicant and pay for college. Today, teens are applying to twelve or more schools. Many of them are considering private or out-of-state colleges. Plus, the cost of college has skyrocketed and acceptance rates are dropping, which forces kids to expand their options. It is not unusual for a teen to spend fifty-plus hours working on their applications. This, on top of their academic and social obligations, makes the process frustrating.

Since starting my business, I have helped hundreds of teens find their perfect college, be able to show what makes them unique, tell their stories in compelling ways, and get accepted to their perfect college with thousands of dollars in scholarships. Nick wanted to attend a private university, but it was not in his family's budget until he got his award letters; he had two full-ride offers. Sydney knew that her education would include grad school, so her goal was to save her college fund to use at that point. She was chosen as a presidential scholar, which meant that her total award package paid for her undergrad education in full.

Once your teen understands what makes them who they are, the rest of the process is much easier. Having an expert guide them through this process can give them amazing insight. You see, when I graduated high school, no one helped me. I have a creative side; I liked fashion and design, so of course I thought that was what I should major in, and thus I started my lustrous college education path. I graduated with a degree in fashion design and hated it — with a capital *Hate*. So I took some time and found me, discovered what I loved and what made me excited to wake up in the morning — thus, the rest of my education.

My passion is to help others discover themselves, even if they change their course along the way. If you know what your core values are, what gets you excited and out of bed in the morning, you are going to be successful. This is about more than college; it is about life. A majority of my clients come in thinking one thing and through the process gain new revelations, like Susan, who thought that she wanted to be a doctor but discovered that marketing was her passion, or Brandon, who had no idea what he wanted to do. But once he found his passion, we put together a perfect college list, which led to eight acceptance letters with over $400,000 in total scholarships.

THE SECRET SAUCE

So what is the secret sauce that makes the students I work with so successful in the process? It's that they understand their U-Niquely-U™ and how to use it in the process. We are seeing more colleges going test-optional and moving to a holistic review process, which means this one ingredient can mean the difference in acceptance or denial, scholarship or no scholarship. This is how they are going to get noticed in the noisy college admission office. Teens move forward by knowing themselves and understanding what they are passionate about, what they believe in, and what they could talk about for hours. This is what I call your U-Niquely-U™, and next to their academic record, I think this is the most important thing students can do.

The purpose in sharing my story is to encourage you — wherever you or your teen are right now, whatever you are going through, good or bad, whatever fears or worries you might have, you can come out on the other side. My business and this process were born out of those dark times in my life. When things were tough and I got a call from someone, asking if I could help, my heart would leap with joy.

Over the years, as parents watched their teens go through the U-Niquely-U™ system, they would say to me, I wish I could do this; I hate my career but don't know what I should do, I can't start a business, I don't have the money to make a change... The list goes on and on. My heart would break. I am the mom who went back to college in her thirties, the woman who sat in tears staring at the fork in the road, knowing that my late husband only had a short time left. I wanted to be there with him for every last moment, but I knew that it was up to me to support myself.

I could have taken the path of a traditional job, and that path would have been perfectly fine. I did consider it, and was offered a few different opportunities. That was my crossroads. And I have never regretted my decision, no matter how hard it was at times.

I am passionate about helping teens find their passion and navigate the college process. I am equally as passionate about helping adults discover what makes them U-Niquely-U™ and step confidently into a calling that they will love, a place where they can make their mark and impact those around them — the one where they will make lifelong friends and have the right opportunities, and that will open doors for them to be successful. Additionally, there is nothing more exciting than seeing someone who is at a fork in the road make a decision to create a new life for themselves.

Maybe you're sitting at a crossroads, wondering what's next. You have a dream, but feel like it's too late to make a change; you worry that you will fail or that you will make the wrong decision. What you need to know is that the battle in your mind is real and your biggest enemy is fear — fear of failure, fear that it's too late, fear that you are making a wrong decision, fear of the unknown, fear of losing everything, fear that if you do nothing you will be stuck in a job you hate, and the fears go on.

Once you take action, you will be able to move from fear to peace and see your dreams become a reality.

Standing at the Crossroads

I will be the first to tell you that the road is not all roses and unicorns. That there are moments when you want to give up. I did not make a million dollars out of the gate, but I stayed the course, I took action, and I never looked back. Finding your strengths and playing to them goes a long way in the journey. I get a lot of calls from families in the spring; they are in tears and panicking that their teen did not get accepted into the schools they applied for, and their only acceptance was at a school they didn't want to attend. They are looking for hope. The sad reality is that there are not a lot of choices at that time, and it is most likely going to cost them time and money. Those teens will have to attend a school they are not right for, make the best of it, and then go through trying to transfer (which is its own beast) or wait a year and go through reapplying all over again.

The same is true in business; many times we think we can't afford to work with an expert or that we can figure it out on our own, and while the school of hard knocks and Google might get you there, it can cost you a lot more than money in the long run. We live in a time where we have access to affordable online education, experts in our field, and resources that would have cost a fortune back in the day. When I am asked why I am so successful, I tell them it's because I did not go it alone; I took action; I know what makes me unique, what my strengths and passions are, and how to use them to create a business that allows me to be authentic and connected.

Your Next Step

Are you standing at a fork in the road, trying to decide what your next step is? You have a choice: go it alone or have an expert in your corner. I want you to know that you don't have to go on this ride alone. You can have someone there holding your hand, telling you to breathe and that it is going to be okay. I got you!

Maybe you're the parent of a college-bound teen and are feeling all the anxiousness of the process. If so, I want to encourage you to check out my book, *College Admissions Secrets: Your Teen's Game Plan to ACE Their Application and Get into Their Dream School.*

Maybe you are standing at your own personal crossroads. It could be that you have a business and need to pivot. Maybe you have a passion and are trying to figure out how to make it a reality. Maybe you're like I was and are at your own crossroads. Then join me at www.drgenalester.life/book for free tools and resources. My system has worked with many clients, and they saw great success. As you can see on my website, it made the process much easier for them. My children used it, as did I with my own business. Across the board, the results warm my heart, and I know there are countless other stories to be shared. My hope in all of this is that through your journey, you are able to say, "Wow, what an amazing ride this has been."

ABOUT GENA LESTER

Dr. Gena Lester is a college admissions expert, speaker, international best-selling author and business coach. She has been guiding families in education and college admissions for over twenty-five years. Dr. Gena is not only a thought leader in the college admissions space but also helps entrepreneurs go from conception to a thriving business. Her background is both education- and psychology-based, which includes a double master's in higher education and I/O psychology, as well as a PhD in Christian Counseling and a doctorate degree in philosophy. Dr. Gena developed the U-Niquely-U™ formula, which she uses to help teens get into the college of their dreams and entrepreneurs find their passions and be more successful on their journey.

Dr. Gena is a professional member of the IECA, HECA, NACAC, NCAG, and TACAC. She works with families both virtually and in person. Dr. Gena can be found on Fox, ABC, *The Morning Blend*, *Flip Your Life*, *Boss Mom*, *College Scoops*, *Nice Guys Business*, and *Motherhood Aligned*, just to name a few.

www.admissionssecrets.com/college-secrets

CHAPTER 5:

SURVIVABILITY
(TODAY AND IN A POST-COVID-19 WORLD)

BY KHALED FATTAL

Never before in human history has man had so much information at his fingertips, and yet never before has he been so misled and misinformed — an unprecedented intervention is critically needed. Time for "real" change!

I was born in Syria, where my dad was a highly prominent journalist, author, and publisher. In fact, my mother's uncle was Nazim al-Qudsi, who was Syria's prime minister numerous times in the '40s and '50s and president in 1961. Nazim was the last democratically elected president of Syria when he was overthrown by a military coup in 1963. The new military rulers started torturing and executing journalists and dissidents. My dad was captured and thrown into prison, awaiting summary execution. His escape from the jaws of death is worthy of a book or a movie. Dad fled over the mountains to Beirut, Lebanon. My mom, sisters, and I followed him a few months later, with no plans to return.

Lebanon was an amazing and most mind-enriching place. The education and experience helped shape my mind and thinking to this day. But once again we were caught in the line of fire as the Lebanese civil war erupted in 1973. Our home was shelled and burned down, and my family needed to flee once again — this time to London, England. I was barely fifteen, yet my life and direction had been profoundly altered twice in less than twelve years.

As a child, I always dreamt of the beaches of Malibu. To many around the world, this was America. It was what we saw in Hollywood movies: a fantasy that never happens. Well, dreams can come true, especially when fate intervenes. In January 1981, I flew into Los Angeles International Airport from London to start attending the University of Southern California in Los Angeles. Embarking on my third life-defining chapter, I would never forget the previous chapters, the perilous journeys my family and I survived, or the values I was reared on.

After graduating college, earning my MBA, and working for international consumer organizations and banking institutions, I found extreme success. However, I felt as though I was still lacking fulfillment. In the mid-'90s, I entered technology and the information superhighway's global infrastructure, its DNS, resiliency, stability, and security. It later became commonly known as the Internet.

I championed, actively led, and contributed at the highest levels in making it the imperfect, multilingual Internet it is today. This was achieved in collaboration with international institutions and forums such as the United Nations (UN), International Telecommunications Union (ITU), Internet Corporation for Assigned Names and Numbers (ICANN), UN Internet Governance Forum (UN IGF), and many other regional and local formats.

My vision was crystal clear: delivering a local and global digital information society that would empower the citizens and make them more informed. The challenge was not only to break down the language barriers of the Internet, which was and is still structured around the ASCII character set (English letters/alphabet), but to turn it into a tool of human empowerment. Yet it was still inaccessible to those whose native languages used different alphabets, such as Japanese, Korean, Arabic, Cyrillic, Chinese, and so forth. My other goals were also to break down cultural barriers and stereotypes for a more tolerant society, improve lives and opportunities, and bring out the humanity in us all.

There was no financial motivation for me. I was neither peddling a digital service nor promoting a business. In truth, I was fortunate to be in such a position. Perhaps that's why I was unwavering and incorruptible.

Remember, these were dinosaur days of the Internet, long before a Syrian brother, Apple's Steve Jobs, truly democratized the Internet with his little finger by inventing apps.

But, to my chagrin, the dream turned into today's nightmare. And without an equally powerful and unprecedented intervention, our democracy will most certainly die.

21ST-CENTURY POISON (1,000 TIMES MORE LETHAL THAN COVID-19, WITH NO VACCINE)

In the last few years, the world has witnessed an unprecedented level of what is commonly referred to as "fake news," false narratives, and misinformation. Many old, new, mainstream, and tech-based news outlets, influencers, bloggers, and social media platforms seem to be held ransom by their advertising budgets and captured by agenda-driven PR companies and lobbyists, along with special interest groups of any bias.

Opposing domestic or international foreign policy narratives and goals with abundant, often limitless, funds started dueling on these channels. Alarmingly, some even became creators of false narratives based on half-truths and twisted facts. Worse yet, most have further transformed into active distributors of these false narratives, becoming merchants of pure lies in their financial pursuit of special interest goals — knowing full well they are actively promoting unfathomable civil unrest and often violence.

Fake news, false narratives, and misinformation are serious and compose part of the "poison" we are all consuming daily. However, without us fully realizing it, the poison has morphed into an unprecedented national and corporate survivability and security threat vector. "Purposed disinformation," however, can bring nations and organizations down to their knees with untold economic and political consequences for lives and livelihoods. Ordinary citizens might see a news story that could be part fact, part disinformation, and conclude that this doesn't impact them, yet that same event can actually be a national security risk to their country and therefore directly affect them.

The noble profession of journalism is expected to provide checks and balances, holding politicians, corporate officials, and others to account. It's also expected to adhere to the highest standards of ethics, integrity, professionalism, authenticity, and above all, objectivity. Today, this critical anchor of any functioning democratic society has been exceptionally, perhaps mortally, compromised. Far too many traditional and modern news media outlets and players have become complicit in spreading this poison, with their flag waving.

The democracy that is enshrined in the West, by law or constitution, and elsewhere, where it is aspired for to serve lives, livelihoods, and people's dreams first and foremost, is under unprecedented threat. Democracy everywhere is in stage four of a fatal cancer, and it is getting worse. It cannot survive without a better-informed citizenry and decision-makers alike.

So, what kind of a new world do you and your children want to live in?

A new economic, political, and democratic world order is materializing at breakneck speed right before our eyes. The powers that be are deeply entrenched and well organized, with plans and narratives to ensure it continues serving them unchanged. Already they are offering their citizens tweaks to the law, cloaked under brilliant slogans of change, as new measures of appeasement to pacify them. They are not offering any substantial reform for the real change needed.

Having worked at and closely observed the highest levels of Internet, national and corporate governance, and policy formulation and implementation, I can tell you that they are all dinosaurs who are inept at serving their citizens or dealing with today's and tomorrow's challenges and threats. Yet the odds are significantly stacked in their favor, as they are successful at rebranding the old world as the new world to maintain the status quo and their continued grip on power.

You might be asking how.

Through the aforementioned poison, they first get us to vote and elect them. There, they control the legislation-making bodies to turn their goals and plans into passed legislation that give their plans and themselves "legality" and "legitimacy." While accomplishing their goals, they continue using the poison; both are a divisive form of distraction. The faces of politicians may change, but notice how perpetual their place in the system is. Their continued grip on power is intended to serve themselves first, not their people. Moreover, once their plans are passed as laws, domestic and international courts and law enforcement agencies must enforce them — asserting their legitimacy further.

The continued success of corrupt and divisive leadership is disastrous for the people. This is one of the reasons why we launched Survivability News™ (in English first, followed by Arabic and other languages), as the home of conflicting news and narratives of opposing camps around the world to offer wider perspectives, unbiased fact-based analysis, and in-depth investigative features. Our quest is to build a tsunami of supporters, citizen journalists, and global collaboration to bring in real change for a better world.

REALITY CHECK: ADAPT OR DIE

For democracy to survive, misled people must be offered a wider perspective on facts to become better informed and engaged citizens — and government and corporate decision-makers who share our values and goals can be instrumental and have a pivotal role to play as well. The model of Survivability News™ allows the citizens to see and engage with conflicting news reports and analysis all in one place. This is further strengthened by special public and private awareness events.

I am fully aware that no one organization or single initiative can save democracy alone. Someone needed to take the uncompromising leadership initiative to break the cycle. I started our unique and imperfect initiative to show that it is possible. I chose to pick up this gauntlet, putting my money where my mouth is.

As a top government or business decision-maker, what's your plan to turn these unprecedented threats into unprecedented competitive advantages and opportunities, now and in the 21st century?

As a citizen, knowing that people are always the ones who pay the price of these failures, will you continue accepting being the constant victim of your politicians and the system's perpetual disasters?

In either case, alternatively:

- Do you share our aspirations?
- Do you want to become part of the solution?
- Will you join us as partners, supporters, or citizen journalists, to make our global collaboration for real change a tsunami and a reality?

As an entrepreneur, I adapted to help others do the same. Here are a few more of my other "cures" for changing the world that you can follow on the Survivability News™ anthology book's dedicated page: https://survivability.news/the-entrepreneurs-cure-how-experts-are-really-changing-the-world/.

- *Survivability*, the book, coming early 2021 with an international book signing tour. For more information, visit https://survivability.news/survivability-the-book-2/

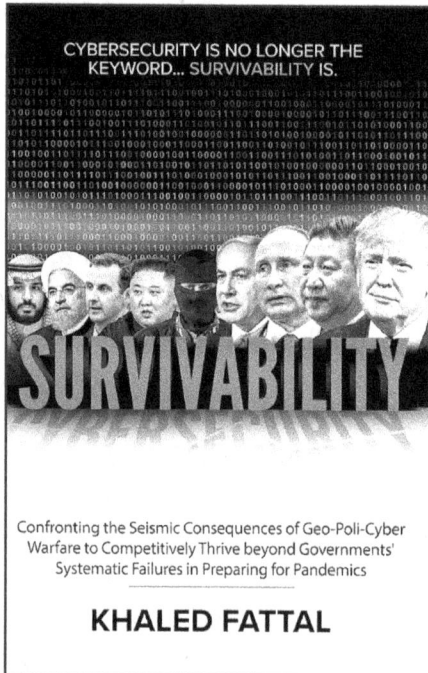

CYBERSECURITY IS NO LONGER THE KEYWORD... SURVIVABILITY IS.

SURVIVABILITY

Confronting the Seismic Consequences of Geo-Poli-Cyber Warfare to Competitively Thrive beyond Governments' Systematic Failures in Preparing for Pandemics

KHALED FATTAL

- My keynote at United Nations WSIS 2019 Global Digital Economy can be found at https://mligrp. com/events/mli-group-chairman-khaled-fattal-statement-at-united-nation-wsis2019-on-the-glob-al-digital-economy-trade-geneva-switzerland/

- MLi Group & Survivability News™ reports, features, virtual round tables, private and public events, and government, board, and C-suite private briefings can be found at https://survivability.news.

- MLi Group's gift to the world — the one minute past midnight 2021 (GMT) launch of Hospitality Sector Survivability, the first in MLi's Sector Survivability Series — can be found at https://survivability.news/sectorsurvivabilityseries/hospitality-2021/

- "Era of the Unprecedented Investigative Program" (2017–18) and VideoCasts (2020) can be found at https://mligrp.com/events/era-of-the-unprecedent-ed-official-release-of-trailer-mli-media-2018/

- "The Quantum Cyber Race – Fallacies of the 'Supremacy Quest' & Threats to Humanity" can be found at https://survivability.news/the-quantum-cy-ber-race-fallacies-of-the-supremacy-quest-threats-to-humanity/

- Nations about to Lose Sovereignty over their own Citizens | How will Ministers & Telecom Regulators Mitigate Becoming Obsolete in 2021? can be found at https://survivability.news/exclusive-na-tions-about-to-lose-sovereignty-over-their-own-cit-izens-how-will-ministers-telecom-regulators-miti-gate-becoming-obsolete-in-2021/

Cybersecurity defenses, structures, and models accepted as gospel are no longer fit for the purposes of defending any fortress today — be it a nation, an organization, or a citizen. Moreover, the necessary regulations are five to ten years too late, and are often watered down to serve special interests or war profiteering before serving the citizen. For every industry sector experiencing technological progress, new vulnerabilities emerge or are created, nurtured, and exploited. As a result, compromised cybersecurity, resiliency, and continuity strategies and solutions keep failing to defend governments and organizations. Yet most of our leaders are satisfied by continuing to follow these failed strategies religiously — and the people they are answerable to are always the ones who pay the price.

Like the universe, the "Era of the Unprecedented" threats haunting our world today are ever-expanding and increasing, and cybersecurity is no longer the keyword — survivability is. To die is not an option, and adapting with agility is key. Although the world you have known will not return to the way you have known it, a small window of opportunity is now open for a better world to emerge. This will not happen without a more active, engaged, and mobilized citizen. More than ever, society needs better-informed decision-makers and leaders with a truer and higher social responsibility ethos.

STAY TUNED! GET ENGAGED!

In 2012, MLi Group was the first organization around the world to identify the early days of ISIS's cyber-destruction plans for the world. This was discovered during a major Internet usability study we conducted across Arabic script communities, to whom we were planning to offer digital services. The discovery was my eureka moment that led me to start creating and formulating MLi's Survivability Strategies, Solutions, and Services to help stakeholders better mitigate looming destructive threats no one was prepared for and to create the terms "Poli-Cyber" and "Geo-Poli-Cyber" to distinguish such attacks from financially motivated cyberattacks.

Today, MLi's first step is delivering ultra-strategic "Survivability" private briefings to chairmen, CEOs, boards, and C-suite and top government officials. A key focus is the influence of geopolitics on the growing seismic shift in the global cyber and non-cyber threat landscape. Evidence is provided as to why current strategies and solutions will continue to fail to defend their "fortresses," followed by discussions on how Survivability Strategies and Solutions are different. There is no sales pitching. When a mindset shift occurs, considerations of new strategies, solutions, and protocols start a snowball effect of holistic implementations, reforms, and restructuring as organic outcomes.

I am often invited to deliver private and public keynotes on similar themes at major expos and summits worldwide, such as the UN WSIS (2019), St. Petersburg Security Summit (2018), and the Abu Dhabi ISNR International Security Expo (2018 and 2020). In December 2020, I appeared on Saudi Arabia's national television live news to discuss its cybersecurity hosting of the G20 virtual meeting by thwarting more than 2.3 million cyberattacks.

New developments are always happening on my side, including MLi's local and international events, initiatives, and related activities. Visit the Survivability News™ dedicated anthology book page for more information and to register to remain up to date.

I invite you to become part of the new solution for a better, fairer global world order.

There is hope. Join us in shaping it.

ABOUT KHALED FATTAL

With a BS in business administration (USC, 1984) and an MBA from CSULA (1987), Khaled Fattal is the founder and chairman of the MLi Group, whose motto is "Cybersecurity Is No Longer the Keyword — Survivability in a Geo-Poli-Cyber" Threatened World Is."

The MLi Group Survivability Strategies™ and Solutions help businesses and governments mitigate the latest cyber and non-cyber threats, especially Geo-Poli-Cyber™ threats whose motivations are political, ideological, extremist, and "religious," which cybersecurity, resiliency, and continuity strategies and solutions routinely fail to defend. A key threat is the destruction/devastation-motivated new breed of GPC hackers and lone wolves, often directed or backed by not only enemies but presumed allies.

The MLi Group and Fattal have been involved in the global infrastructure of the Internet and its resiliency, stability, and security since the mid-'90s; he championed it as and led the way in making it the multilingual Internet it is today through international institutions and forums such as the UN, ITU, ICANN, UN IGF, and many others.

Fattal is frequently invited to speak at and chair public and private expos and international conferences and events. He is regularly interviewed on radio and TV, and he often writes for cyber, Internet, political, and defense publications.

CHAPTER 6:

DISCOVERING PEACE
WITHIN AND WITH OTHERS
(THE FAITH-MINDED CURE!)

BY KIM REUTZEL

It was 1997, the day after Princess Diana died. My husband and I were on our way home from a family gathering when I first experienced a weird feeling that made me think I was having a heart attack. The more I thought about it, the worse I felt. As we drove through each town, I wondered, "Should I stop at this town's emergency room?" Sweaty hands, shortness of breath, stomachache, dizziness, and what seemed to feel like electricity going through my body frightened me.

I made it home, and over the next few months discovered the problem: I was having anxiety attacks. These anxiety attacks stemmed from a bad internal relationship I had with myself from faulty programs in my subconscious that overwhelmingly affected my relationship with myself and others. I realized that the relationship I had with myself and with God was definitely spilling over into all other relationships in my life. If your mental life with yourself and God are not healthy, then it's quite possible your relationships with others will be affected as well.

So what exactly have I found out over the last twenty-plus years that has changed my life to the core? There are so many things I could share, but here are a few that my clients and I have benefited from the most.

KNOW WHO YOU ARE

You have been given special gifts from God to fulfill His will throughout your life, and they are good. "I am fearfully and wonderfully made" (Ps. 139:14). Know this: He has made each one of us differently, and there is no "normal" out there to try to achieve. "What we have is one body with many parts, each its proper size and in its proper place." (1 Cor. 12) You are the only person to be who God created you to be! So stop trying to fit into some man-made mold you or someone else has created for you, and know that it is beneficial to give this freedom to others as well. Knowing we were all made differently can create compassion for others' weaknesses and build an understanding that we all have different things we need to work on and are talented in. Allow yourself to be "you" and others to be who God created them to be, and when you do this, you will be attracted to and attract 100 percent of your God-designated people to you.

I believe we all have different temperaments to fulfill our God-given purpose, but yet we are all alike in the fact that we all need to be loved, sufficient, and safe. It seems as though most of our problems in life are caused by trying to meet these needs by worldly temptations and ungodly ways, which can then cause stress, hurt, indifference, and conflict in our internal and interpersonal relationships.

I believe we were made to get each of these needs met from God. Let's face it: in this fallen world, anyone can reject you, but no one gets to define you unless you let them — don't let them! Free yourself from overvaluing others' opinions, and release others from your idea of who they should be as well! Everyone has different temperaments, characteristics and life experiences that have formed them into who they are and how they respond to these fallen-world situations. Some people realize there is a better way, yet don't know how to get it, and others we live with have no clue that another way to get their needs met exists at all.

THE BIBLE AND NEUROSCIENCE

God designed our minds to help us conserve energy by automating repeated thoughts. He asked you to meditate on His promises so that they will be automated to bring you peace. Satan tries to trick us to meditate on our worries: "...[B]e watchful. Your adversary the devil prowls around like a roaring lion, seeking someone to devour." (1 Peter 5:8) He tricks us into programming past trauma experiences that don't provide us peace in our loving God as He intended. These programs work automatically in your subconscious mind, and they need to be reprogrammed with new Godly-promised thoughts. "Take captive every thought and purpose captive to the obedience of Christ." (2 Cor. 10:5) God directs you to Him to receive these downloads that will truly make the difference you have been trying hard to find. "Peace I leave with you; My peace I give to you; not as the world gives do I give to you. Do not let your heart be troubled, nor let it be afraid." (John 14:27)

Your brain is simply trying to keep you safe. Your brain does not know the difference between a lie or truth; it believes what you record over and over again. Replace thoughts that bring unease with Godly-designed loving truths. "Finally, brothers and sisters, whatever is true, whatever is noble, whatever is right, whatever is pure, whatever is lovely, whatever is admirable — if anything is excellent or praiseworthy — think about such things." (Phil. 4:8) Please know that God provides all you need, and that you were intended to get your needs met from Him rather than being tricked into trying to get it from others or earthly things. God's promises are your source of love, sufficiency, and safety. Meditate on His loving words day and night rather than focusing on your worries or others' words.

LOVING SCRIPTURES OFFER YOU PEACE

This is one of the things that helped me change my unwanted thoughts of anxiety to peace. Your God loves you and wants you to have all His best. Looking at His Word as your guiding grace and a beautiful place to get mind/thought principles is one way to take away uncertainty or wishy-washy feelings that cause distress. "For the word of God is living and active and full of power." (Heb. 4:12) Transferring unwanted beliefs of yourself and others, formed from what you recorded from past events, is a good place to start, and it helps to know your loving God is helping and supporting you in love. "... for I am your God. I will strengthen you and help you . . ." (Is. 41:10)

My dear friend, I want you to know that it is through your spirit that you have contact with your Heavenly God. Your God-given spirit is the deepest part of your existence and was created by God to contact and receive His love. I benefit greatly by setting aside a quiet time for God each day, and I would love you to experience this peace and joy as well. This is when He can be heard by your soul (mind, will, emotions, and awareness), when your earthly desires and worries are quieted, and you are able to focus on Him and His benefits only.

A HEAVENLY MINDSET

No matter what happens right now, say to yourself, "I will be in heaven and with my loved ones and God someday. I will understand the things I don't understand now." Remember the verse: "Set your mind and keep focused habitually on the things above [the heavenly things], not on things that are on the earth [which have only temporal value]." (Col. 3:2) This will free you from being paralyzed in any present unwanted circumstances. Know that you can have struggles in this life, but be confident. The Bible says, "be of good cheer, take heart; I have overcome the world." (John 16:33) Focus on the promises you already have in Christ rather than your worries, because when you know You are His, bought and paid for with His blood, you can decide everything from this knowledge and stop participating in this world as though the need is still there to get confidence from something or someone.

KINDNESS TO YOURSELF AND OTHERS

You have heard the saying that "hurt people hurt people." Yet also know that hurt people hurt themselves and react to things in the only way they know how to because they have automated, untrue, and unhealthy beliefs that were programmed from earlier events in their lives. These subconscious neurons create feelings, words, and reactions that are no longer helping them. It is not done intentionally; it is simply a result of unhealthy beliefs that cause unhealthy feelings and reactions that one's brain initially programmed to keep them safe. It was what they felt would protect them at that time. It was done using earthly interpretations of what would help rather than God's promises, and it was cleverly schemed by our enemy to keep them and us from God's beautiful plan and peace. This leaves us trying to prove and protect things that God already gave us. The unfortunate thing is that we give this value to others by valuing what they say or do more than what God's promises provide. We can forgive others in love by knowing God created us all in His image and He wants us all in heaven with Him.

But it is also important to put up boundaries to others' fallen-world behaviors that are unhealthy to you. I call it boundaries wrapped in love. We can still love and forgive the person God created. So when you are drawn into others' unhealthy situations of sin, pray for them; ask God to reveal to them what needs to be revealed to them and ask God to show you what He wants you to see about this as well. Value who a person is in Christ and resist valuing or reacting to their bad behaviors or words. Create healthy boundaries wrapped in love. "Bear one another's burdens, and so fulfill the law of Christ." (Gal. 6:2) "Beloved, let us love one another: for love is of God." (1 John 4:7)

Another way to keep a humble and kind heart is to choose gratitude on purpose. Gratitude and hate cannot live together in your mind! Each moment, you choose one or the other. Remembering a few good things a "hard to get along with" person does is very helpful in times when you are upset with them. Remembering that God is quick to forgive us, it is best to be quick to forgive others before Satan gets a foothold in your mind. This does not mean a "wrong" is "right"; it means we allow God's creation to move forward as He planned in love.

Know that God will turn what was meant for bad into something good. Resist the temptation of "getting even" with those that wronged you. Love the "who" and devalue the "do" in your mind. "Don't say 'I'll avenge that wrong!' Wait on the LORD and he will deliver you." (Prov. 20:22) Remember we are all sinners and fall short and are saved by Christ. "[F]or all have sinned and fall short of the glory of God." (Rom. 3:23) "I am he who blots out your transgressions, for my own sake, and remembers your sins no more." (Is. 43:25) Life is hard and we all have our own temptations, yet it is such a blessing to know that God provided for them all. I no longer sit in sorrow of my sins; I accept fully the gift provided even while I still make mistakes, and you must too. Your God is love!

EXPECTATIONS: BE UNOFFENDABLE

Do your best to be unoffendable in this fallen world. Know you have an enemy that will use other people to get to you, just like he tried to with Jesus. "The thief comes only in order to steal and kill and destroy. I came that they may have and enjoy life, and have it in abundance." (John 10:10)

Now, 1997 seems as though it were eons ago. Extreme anxiety is only a memory for me now. Do I have moments when I start to think wrong thoughts? Of course! Feelings seem strong, yet I know from neuroscience that our feelings follow our thoughts. Challenges still exist more than ever in today's world, yet I know that you can move above your feelings and stand strong in knowing you can change a thought that created an unwanted feeling by a few brain reprogramming techniques that neuroscience suggests, which also line up with what Scripture taught so many years ago.

May you be blessed by starting with this prayer process for those times you catch yourself thinking in wrong ways about yourself or others:

> Say to yourself in prayer: *(submit to God)* "Jesus help me," *(resist the Devil)* "I reject that thought as not mine," *(meditate on God's word)* "I replace it with _____," *(give thanks to the Lord)* "thank You, Lord!" (James 4:7, Psalms 1:2, and 1 Thessalonians 5:18)

Could you make a decision today to take captive the thoughts that do not line up with God's promises … and throw them out? May God bless you as you live life to the fullest while being surrounded in His love, because you choose to receive the free gift He provided to you … it is yours already. Amen!

ABOUT KIM REUTZEL

Kim Reutzel is the publisher of *WomenInc. Magazine* and a best-selling author, speaker, mentor/coach and teacher. She received her master's degree in clinical Christian counseling in 2001. Now working on her doctorate degree and specializing in Biblical temperament therapy and neuroscience, Kim can't wait to support you in living your best life in whatever way she can through her books, courses, teachings, and coaching. Kim has been featured on *The 700 Club*, *The Harvest Show*, and hundreds of radio stations as a featured guest. For more information about Kim's classes, coaching, or books, go to www.kimandfaith.com (a special gift awaits as well — "Scripture Hugs," a twelve-day devotional); for daily inspiration, follow Kim on Facebook at www.facebook.com/kimandfaith.

CHAPTER 7:

INTANGIBLE LEGACY
(BREAKTHROUGH INNOVATIONS IN VIDEO GAMES AND BEYOND)

BY MICHAEL CHANG

A lifelong dreamer, I immersed myself early on in iconic games like *Pac-Man, Oregon Trail,* and *Duke Nukem.* In particular, I've always been fascinated by video games which trigger strong human emotions like pride, sadness, fear, empathy, and joy. Professionally, I found my calling in marketing software and video games that address underlying human needs. These ranged from idle simulation games targeting moms and kids to strategy, sports, and role-playing games targeting teens, young professionals, and dads.

While counseling a conflicted educator-parent at the ISTE Conference in Chicago, the idea for my book was born. I'm setting out to address these questions head-on:

- What is it *really* like to create and publish games?

- Does the industry offer viable opportunities for young people? What about teens who are not STEM-inclined or artistic?

- And should parents and educators foster or cure such "dreamers"? And if the former, *how?*

My book was only made possible with invaluable, candid perspectives from some of my most admired colleagues in the video game industry. Over a dozen experts were interviewed, and the following are some of the noteworthy highlights.

On the words of wisdom she would offer her former twelve-year-old self about a career in the video game industry, if she could go back in time:

> 1. "Don't believe the hype.
>
> 2. Stay curious.
>
> 3. Sweat the UX most of all."
>
> — Christine Woertink, SVP of product, Age of Learning/ABCmouse

On the keys to success in the video game industry, to aspiring game designers, developers, marketers, and publishers:

> "Find a mentor if you can, someone that is genuinely interested in helping people and sharing their experiences. With a mentor you can do some course correction, and figure out your long-term goals."
>
> — Julia Kenny, content and partnerships manager, SEGA Europe

On getting started in the video game industry:

> "I was working in a consulting firm, assisting with M&A when I realized that there was actually a lot of money in my hobby. As soon as I realized that people like me (non-artistic, non-coders) were still useful, I made sure that every project I worked on was somehow related to technology or gaming or entertainment."
>
> — Max Sloan, market and competitive intelligence manager at King (Activision Blizzard)

On what he does in the video game industry, and what keeps him up at night:

"As a producer I do my best to build, inspire and grow teams to make the impossible possible. What keeps me up at night is not what the industry is doing today, but where I feel the trend is going tomorrow and the day after that. I'm always thinking about what's next."

— Jeff Skalski, COO and executive producer, Yellow Brick Games

On the one video game legend (living or otherwise) who he would have dinner with, and why:

"Hironobu Sakaguchi, the creator of *Final Fantasy*. Those games all bring larger-than-life scenarios that effectively tap into the corners of our minds in interesting ways, whether that be through a socially relevant undertone, its odd and interesting characters, or dynamic ways in which it presents its worlds. I'd like to try and fit his personality to the games that he brought to life."

— Jason Millena, senior creative director, Behaviour Interactive

Professionally, I advise, consult, and/or invest in promising video game developers and tech startups to help them tell captivating stories and hyper-grow. To democratize the art and science of game and app marketing, I love sharing best practices through my blog, *Videogame. marketing.*

With this chapter, I would like to celebrate the entrepreneurs doing amazing things. I genuinely believe that for most video game developers and entrepreneurs creating consumer products, there are always two answers to one critically important question.

What defines success for a video game or consumer product?

The common answer — the one taught in business schools across the world — focuses on the hard tangibles. These entail financial success, which means achieving and exceeding targets in acquiring players and users and maximizing revenue and profits.

The less common answer provokes more discussions and debates. Arguably, the intangible legacy or lasting success of a video game or consumer product is measured by the number of people who are touched and transformed by the experience.

With a focus on the latter, I want to celebrate the visionaries behind Everydae, Virtuleap, and Fusion Odyssey.

Christine Outram of Everydae is transforming traditional college and SAT prep into something highly interactive, fun and bite-sized. In Virtuleap, Amir Bozorgzadeh is using virtual reality brain training games to reverse the effects of aging-related cognitive degeneration. Chris Thomas's Fusion Odyssey system uses sports psychology to help youth athletes take full ownership and hack the emotional, psychological, and intellectual elements of the mental game, in order to execute personal bests on the playing field and in life.

CHRISTINE OUTRAM

In the hypercompetitive world of college admissions stand time-tested pillars. They stand in times of global prosperity and in times of economic hardships. Together with the GPA, the SAT is an objective, concrete measure of academic aptitude. Ubiquitous and recognized names like Kaplan, Princeton Review, and the Educational Testing Service resonate with many students. They are giants whose services and products have decided for generations — and decide still — whether a young man or woman gains admission, or not. By his or her first-string schools ... or their backups.

These test preparation programs are both revered and daunting. SAT prep is a critical step, never to be taken lightly. Commanding over $200 for one hour of private tutoring, premium prep services can come with guaranteed high scores. Catering to the economically privileged, such services are priced befitting their perceived weight in gold.

As digital-native, attention span-challenged Generation Z comes of age, so too has SAT prep. Everydae, a Santa Monica-based startup, has taken SAT learning and preparation and made it accessible and palatable.

For table stakes, Everydae helps students learn and practice problem-solving, reading comprehension, critical writing, and more on the go. Everydae fits, by design, seamlessly with a student's life. Where the student goes, the Everydae app goes. Think on public transit, in flight, between classes, during lunch break ... and yes, as with a live tutor, students get instant feedback with each problem.

Everydae's CEO, Christine Outram, was named a Top 100 IOT thinker and one of the thirty-six most creative women by Business Insider. She is the inventor of the electric bike known as the Copenhagen Wheel, a *TIME* Magazine Best Invention.

Particularly novel is Everydae's design philosophy, inspired by its CEO's own player experience with games like *Donkey Kong*, *The Sims*, and *Candy Crush Saga*. Much like gold coins or cartoon mushrooms turning magically into shape-shifting superpowers, students are treated to unexpected rewards. Sandwiched between discussions about the main ideas in passages or the theories of protein synthesis, students are quizzed by "Extra Credit" questions.

To reinvent an otherwise laborious prep experience, Everydae designed snackable "moments of joy and delight." In this case, some extra credit questions educate teens about career choices — for example, about the function and average starting salary for an architect or an actuary. Others test students on their knowledge of pop culture or topical events.

Priced at $39 a month or $179 for lifetime use, Everydae makes SAT prep affordable. Adopted broadly, Everydae can be a true equalizer.

By equalizing access to high-quality education and tutoring services, Everydae has the potential to democratize an entire industry — not to mention changing the lives of thousands upon thousands of young people.

AMIR BOZORGZADEH

Handsome and slender, Amir Bozorgzadeh looks like he walked off the cover of *Cyberpunk 2077*. Long a fan of "thinking man's games," Amir immersed himself in games like *Total Annihilation* and *Starcraft*. Such games appeal to strategic, analytical thinkers who rely more on resource optimization in combat rather than trigger-quick twitch reflexes.

As the CEO of a technology startup in Lisbon, Portugal, Amir is on a mission. Channeling the real-time strategy (RTS) games of his youth, Amir is applying the analytical gameplay to solving a different set of real-world problems. Virtuleap positions itself as a health and education virtual reality startup, dedicated to elevating the cognitive assessment and training industry through virtual reality and artificial intelligence.

Virtuleap has created a suite of brain training mini-games such as *Magic Deck, Memory Wall, Hide & Seek, Pizza Builder*, and more. Instead of idle gaming made solely for entertainment, these games train a range of cognitive functions like memory, problem-solving, spatial orientation, and more.

Alzheimer's and Parkinson's, two neurodegenerative diseases that most commonly affect people over the ages of 60–65, affect an estimated 50 million and 10 million people respectively worldwide.[4] But does brain training work? To address this question on the minds of cognitive researchers and trainers, Amir's response is refreshingly concise: let the data be the proof in the pudding. His product philosophy is equally simple — tightly integrate product development and research validation.

For example, after playing Virtuleap's *Memory Wall*, do the subjects remember grocery lists better? For those playing spatial orientation games, can they recall the names and faces of loved ones? Furthermore, do people who have mastered the *Pizza Builder* game see measurably better hand-eye coordination in golf or tennis?

Virtuleap's first paying client partner? The American Association of Retired Persons (AARP). Though long sales cycles in a regulated industry, Amir's Virtuleap is just getting started. And if it does work?

For 60 million people across the world, Virtuleap can be the missing piece of the puzzle to turn back the clock and start slowing or undoing the effects of cognitive degeneration.

With many of my video game projects, we talk about activating strong human emotions (of joy, sadness, anger, empathy, or pride) or activating players' deeply-rooted needs (for love, power, wealth, social connection, etc.) — en route to achieving financial success.

Rather than focusing on financial metrics, mission-driven entrepreneurs (video game developers, app entrepreneurs, or coach-consultants) focus on touching and transforming lives. This brings us to our next visionary who dares to change the world.

CHRIS THOMAS

It is also along the second dimension where Chris Thomas, the owner and CEO of Fusion Odyssey, radiates and shines. Chris is a Super Bowl champion, former standout wide receiver in the NFL, performance development mentor, and motivational speaker. Neither a video game nor a technology startup, *why* Fusion Odyssey will become apparent shortly.

---

4. "What Is Parkinson's?", European Parkinson's Disease Association (EPDA), accessed January 24, 2021, https://www.epda.eu.com/about-parkinsons/what-is-parkinsons/.

Let us start with Chris's question to each of his athletes:

Could you perform where your dream hinged on one moment?

To any game designer or producer audacious enough to even attempt to touch and transform lives, this is next-gen and aspirational. To help a fellow man or woman achieve a lifelong dream? That is life-changing, defined and personified.

While sports psychology and simulation training are commonly used in sports at the elite levels of competition, Fusion Odyssey goes many steps further — like leapfrogging from tabletop games to immersive virtual reality.

Chris's Fusion Odyssey system allows athletes to take full, trusted ownership around tapping into the emotional, psychological, and intellectual elements of the mental game.

To create a direct pathway to a "mental connection," athletes are asked to start by visualizing the specific action required to create a specific desired result. Once the mental connection and the technical proficiency (required to execute precisely what the mind has visualized, through repetition and practice) are in place, athletes are now empowered to "own" the action with 100 percent confidence.

The psychological game allowed athletes to play in a cocoon free from the fear of failure, judgment, and pressure. By randomly introducing stressful situations during practice (for example, catching a weighted football with one's eyes closed), the player learns to quiet his/her inner self-talk, accept imperfection as human, trust in his/her preparedness, and hyperfocus the mind and body to executing the play at hand — whether that be a high-stakes play during a game or a stressful practice situation, *whenever* that arises.

Like a chess match or the World Series of Poker, the intellectual game requires a player to diligently study an opponent, recognize subtle patterns and weaknesses (some of which only emerge as the game progresses), choose the right moment to explode, outmaneuver, and execute a perfect breakout play for the highlight reel. And then do exactly that consistently, over and over again.

The end result? Chris's athletes are able to reach and consistently perform at levels never seen before on the field.

When interviewed, each and every one of Chris's athletes attests to both the breakthrough performance he or she was able to achieve on the field and their ensuing success in high school, college … and in life.

CONSTANT LIGHT

To me, unlocking the keys to helping people realize their full human potential — through education, games, sports, and otherwise — is truly touching and transformative, and nothing short of divine. For these reasons, I am humbled and inspired by the stories of such incredible entrepreneurs like Christine, Amir, Chris, and more, who are on a mission to change lives and make the world a better place. This chapter is dedicated to them.

As someone who sifts through mountains of information and data in search of heretofore undiscovered gems to help entrepreneurs and creatives change the world, I believe it is our responsibility to *be* the constant beacon of light, shining all the more brilliantly, *especially* in confusing, uncertain, challenging times.

For the greater book *Video Game Careers Demystified: The Trifecta of Creators, Athletes, and Ecosystem in a Thriving Industry*, I want to express genuine gratitude for the generously contributed perspectives and words of wisdom from esteemed video game professionals and colleagues. My heartfelt gratitude goes to Christine Woertink of Age of Learning, Martin Caplan of Amber, Ravi Gogte of Logitech, Davis Kurzenski of Unity Technologies, Julia Kenny of SEGA Europe, Jason Millena of Behaviour Interactive, Max Sloan of Activision Blizzard, Ray Salloom of Scalarr, Kate Edwards of Geogrify, Jeff Skalski of Yellow Brick Games, Hossein Jalali of Virtuleap, and Chris Hockabout of Cloud Chamber.

ABOUT MICHAEL CHANG

A technology nerd and brand/category maker, Michael Chang loves spotting "tipping points" (using structured research) to tell powerful stories and create laser-focused activation. As a marketing practitioner and consultant, Michael has had the pleasure of commercializing emerging technology for software companies like Autodesk, PubMatic, and Citrix — and defining bleeding-edge consumer behavior for video game publishers such as RockYou, Jagex, and EA. Michael enjoys solving tough problems — by blending the business rigor of the Fortune 1000 with the agility and passion of startup founders — to grow minds, brands, revenue, and value.

His book, *Video Game Careers Demystified: The Trifecta of Creators, Athletes, and Ecosystem in a Thriving Industry*, informs and educates young gamers with a "God's-eye view" of what it's really like to develop and publish games. By quoting experts who worked on icons like *Halo*, *Assassin's Creed*, *Battlefield*, and ABCmouse.com — as well as entrepreneurs reinventing education, health care, and youth sports through gamification — the book encourages young people to look within themselves and to explore turning their passions into lifelong pursuits in gaming, the arts, technology, and beyond.

CHAPTER 8:

TREASURE, TECHNOLOGY, OR . . .?

BY MARC GERIENE AND KRIST GERIENE

A MISSION STATEMENT AND THE SEARCH FOR A BUSINESS IDENTITY

In 1996, Nova Marine Exploration Inc. had been in business for three years. We were commercial divers, submersible remotely operated vehicle (ROV) pilots, shipwreck exploration adventurers, treasure hunters, partners, *and* brothers. We had also begun prototyping our concepts for what became a series of patentable inventions. With so many business facets for such a young company, we lacked clarity and, most of all, a distinct identity. As a company, what was Nova Marine Exploration, and what did we want it to become?

So we hired a consultant, someone who knew us pretty well but was not very familiar with the nature of our business. After a couple of hours exchanging questions and answers, followed by a couple more hours of mostly arduous and grueling "clearing" exercises, we finally came up with the first mission statement for our company. It read:

> "To chart a new course of exploration and discovery
> in a way that challenges the industry, with innovative
> alliances of relationships and technology, in order to

> elevate the individual awareness toward historical,
> environmental and human concerns."

One single meeting, with a talented individual counseling us, effectively created enough clarity for us to identify our newly emerging management objectives. It also led us to change the name and the direction of our company, and subsequently our business model. Ultimately, we began focusing more on innovation, with the intent of developing new hydrodynamic designs for submersible robotics systems or underwater drones. Soon we were applying for, and receiving, design and utility patents from the US Patent and Trademark Office as well as international patents for the arcuate-wing Nova Ray® ROV.

Nova Ray® ROV

Our new company, Nova Ray, Inc., entered its first marine technology trade show with expectations of congratulations and kudos — or at least some kind of appreciation. As it turned out, when you challenge the status quo of an industry, you should not expect to make new friends. Instead, you will more likely lose some old friends. And if you expect to be a disruptive force in your industry, you cannot afford to be sensitive in what ultimately may become a hostile environment

— otherwise you will miss the real opportunities! Your competitors will try to invalidate you, and even the clients may invalidate you, until you illustrate the opportunity you are offering them, as it applies to their bottom line. Then the change kicks in and the validation emerges in the form of new business and more profitability.

When the Nova Ray® ROV, integrated with cameras and various imaging sensors, was introduced to clients for underwater oil and gas pipeline inspections, it proved to be seven times more efficient than any other combination of similarly applied technologies and field techniques at the time. The impact of this new invention with its relative applications, combining existing technologies for greater profit to the client, was enough to earn a three-person company in Kirkland, Washington, a multimillion-dollar patent licensing, technology transfer, and R&D contract with PETRONAS, the national oil company of Malaysia. Ultimately, our mission statement and our conscious choice to challenge the status quo through "innovative alliances of relationships and technology" raised the awareness of the industry, changed the expectations of the clients, and eventually raised the performance bar for the competition.

CREATING A LEGACY THROUGH TEACHING

"You teach best what you most need to learn."
— Richard Bach, *Illusions*

"Whether it's the best of times or the worst of times,
it's the only time we've got."
— Art Buchwald

Up until our first patent license contract, we had been identified mostly as commercial divers, ROV pilots, and shipwreck-treasure hunters. As a result of our business deal with PETRONAS, we were then elevated to the status of inventors and international businessmen. Throughout the process of developing a technology and building a successful business with an international clientele, we had incorporated a disciplined, weekly routine for management by objectives, or goal-setting, which actually worked! The financial success of our twelve-year innovation project, from inception to completion, was proof that our management system for setting and achieving our goals was successful as well. This was too good to limit it to ourselves and not share it, so we decided to write a book.

We had no experience in writing a book; however, we had a lot of experience with not letting inexperience stop us. We had always embraced each opportunity, no matter how large or small, as a treasure hunt. Every stage of innovation, from the initial prototype to the commercial model of the Nova Ray®, involved planning, financing, negotiations, legal filings, leasing office and warehouse space, hiring personnel, staging, marketing, and production, all of which are integral to business development; however, we preferred to treat each of those objectives as an event in a series of treasure hunts. It worked so well for us, we still use it today with every project, no matter how large or small. Though the self-help book market is a crowded field, the message we chose had a slightly different approach: to transform goal-setting into the search for one's own treasure. We dove into writing the book like every other project we had undertaken as partners, without fear of failure, and then looked for a lifeline afterwards. Fortunately for us, we found a good publisher and with great guidance — boom! We wrote a successful book with Best Seller Publishing, *Finding Your Treasure Without Losing Yourself*.

> **Excerpt from the book *Finding Your Treasure Without Losing Yourself* (Chapter 4, "Creating Your Treasure Map with the Ten Cs")**
>
> You need a map. You must have a map. Maps are a great catalyst from which to launch an adventure! Have you ever seen a treasure movie or read a treasure story without a map? In fact, the map is what draws everybody into the picture, both in art and in life, and makes us either want to watch or want to play.

In the movies, someone usually has the map or has found a map, which becomes the focus for the plot to develop and the characters to participate. In most cases, somebody else created the treasure map. In your treasure hunt, however, you need to create your own treasure map. You are the artist and the adventurer, and you have to design, draw, or sketch your treasure map for others to want to participate with you in your treasure hunt. Since it is your map, you get to make it any way you want: the more exciting, the better!

Here is where the fun begins! I mean, it should be really fun! Remember, we have enough work, boredom, and drudgery in our lives. If your treasure hunt is compelling and exciting enough, then others will want to join you when you invite them. You can tell them about your treasure, and you can tell them how much fun they will have; however, people love images, pictures, and video, so remember that when you begin sketching your treasure map. The vivid imagery you create with your efforts is what will be most effective and will draw other people to participate with you.

Just as in the old treasure stories, where the adventurers sailed the seven seas, you will want to navigate through the characteristics or the "Ten Cs," which will assist you in building your comprehensive, fun, and exciting treasure map.

The Ten Cs are Clarity, Change, Conviction, Commitment, Consistency, Confidence, Credibility, Compatibility, Cleanse, and Contrast. Over the next ten chapters, we will examine each one of these characteristics and how you can create exciting images for your treasure map, so you can begin your own treasure hunt.

(end of excerpt)

For us, our book was another step in the progression of the development of our identity, much like receiving patents on the Nova Ray®. You're just an idea person until your first patent is granted; then you are an *inventor*. You can talk about writing a book, as many people do; after it is published, though, you are an *author*. Expectations change around you, and reactions from readers are both fulfilling and rewarding.

The most rewarding part of publishing the book has been the dividends received in emails and letters from readers who tell us how much our book helped them accomplish their dreams and goals. Raising awareness of the importance of living each day to its fullest is fundamental to raising the quality of our lives and changing the world in a positive way. The knowledge that many people have taken those steps towards success through the information shared in our book is worth more than money to us!

Since our first book was a success, we decided to launch another "teaching document" in the second quarter of 2021, titled *Finding Your Treasure Through Inventions, Patents and Licensing©*. This book will guide the reader from the initial concept phase to the point where the inventor lets go, benefiting from our experiences and expertise in the development and monetizing of patents, trademarks, and technological know-how.

INSPIRATION AND THE "TREASURE EXPERIENCE SOCIETY™"

Throughout history, the mystery and excitement of shipwrecks and sunken treasures has captured our imagination and inspired dreams of grand adventure and discovery. The excitement and fun of looking for the treasure is rewarding to almost all of the participants, even when the expeditions end without success.

We have turned our dreams into reality, and adventure into a science that often takes us deep below the ocean's surface into a realm where few dare to venture. We have travelled the globe searching for lost and sunken ships and turned them into opportunities to resurrect history and solve mysteries from the past.

As early as our first expedition, we have encountered people who wished they could go too but were resigned to the fact that the treasure-hunting business was more ideally suited for unattached individuals with no personal, financial, or career obligations. Over the past forty years, we have encountered hundreds of people of all persuasions and walks of life with obligations and commitments that kept them from joining us on our expeditions.

Today, we are fortunate enough to be able to balance our lives and commitments with ongoing research and development of new patents for our underwater drones and applying them to the field application of shipwreck exploration and treasure hunting. So we can be reasonably assured of the financial rewards from the periodic sale or license of patents to make up for potential losses while searching for sunken ships.

Shipwreck exploration and new discoveries, presented through the Internet and social media, provide the infrastructure for the seamless delivery of "live" information and entertainment and the "virtual experience" of participating in new discoveries, through the website www.yourtreasureexperience.com. Adventurers and explorers at heart may join the "Treasure Experience Society™" without giving up their day-to-day lives and responsibilities in the process. The Treasure Experience Society™ activities will not be limited to the field of commercially viable shipwrecks for recovery; instead, projects will be selected based upon the "excitement factor," the historical impact, the academic value to archaeologists, and public interest in the subject.

THE TREASURE EXPERIENCE SOCIETY™ MISSION STATEMENT

"We explore the unsolved mysteries of history in search of projects that challenge our understanding about what's possible so that anyone can have permission to live their dreams."

What is possible? And who decides that for us? We are living in a world that changes faster than ever, learning that what was not possible a few years ago may be easily accomplished today. Yet we still experience our own form of self-limiting actualization, mostly in what we let ourselves believe.

Our new mission is to challenge as many people as possible to "live their dreams" while we pursue our own. After all, we have had so much excitement in our endeavors that we want everybody else to experience the same fulfillment.

Twenty-four years ago, we challenged the submersible ROV industry with the invention of the Nova Ray® technology, and as a result, many changes to the way business was completed ensued. In our first mission statement, with little understanding at the time, we declared that we would create innovative alliances. And we did! After all, what could be more innovative than a three-person company in Washington State creating international business relationships in Japan, Singapore, and Malaysia, as in the case with PETRONAS — the national oil company of Malaysia?

Today, with the Treasure Experience Society™, we are now challenging each and every member to live their lives to the fullest. Any worthwhile endeavor will very likely encounter resistance or setbacks. We have endured resistance and setbacks in the form of severe weather conditions, mechanical failures, and human error and failures in the short term; however, we have continuously sought to overcome the obstacles that would keep us from our success, and we will continue to share our solutions with anyone who is interested. Share in our excitement and make it yours at www.yourtreasureexperience.com.

ABOUT MARC AND KRIST GERIENE

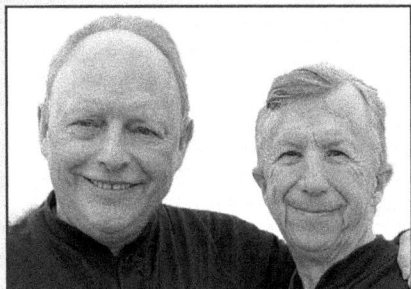

The two brothers signed onto their first expedition in 1978 to locate a 17th-century Spanish galleon that was lost on a reef known as Silver Shoals, eighty miles north of Hispaniola in the Caribbean. That decision changed the course of both of their lives, from their intended professions as an attorney and a doctor to commercial divers and adventurers who have participated in and led more than twenty expeditions from the Alaskan Arctic to Florida and from the Caribbean to Japan and the Philippines.

Marc and Krist have been credited with the discovery of an early 12th-century Chinese (Sung Dynasty) shipwreck in the South China Sea, colonial period Spanish, British, and American ships in the Caribbean Sea, the Gulf of Mexico, and the Atlantic Ocean, and Imperial Japanese shipwrecks from World War II. They have converted some of their discoveries to successful recoveries, resulting in museum collections of shipwreck artifacts.

As business partners, they have converted many of their failed expeditions to innovations as co-inventors of ten international and U.S. patents, some of which were licensed to a Fortune 100 company. They also co-authored the self-help/adventure book *Finding Your Treasure Without Losing Yourself.*

CHAPTER 9:

HOW TO EARN A FORTUNE
(AN ENTREPRENEUR SHARES THE GREATEST ADVICE
HE EVER RECEIVED IN BUSINESS SCHOOL)

BY CHRISTOPHER MUSIC, MBA, RFC, CBEC

I attended Kent State University in 1990–91 to earn an MBA with the hopes and dreams of becoming a successful entrepreneur in the world of personal financial planning. Little did I know that the MBA overall did little to prepare me for the real world of owning and running a business, for, you see, academia teaches business students to be employees and not business leaders — what corporate donors are interested in training new competition? But there was one moment…

It was in the spring of 1991, on a chilly Tuesday afternoon. I was taking an economics course which really amounted to a study of advanced calculus applied to the price and quantity of goods and services. Not too exciting for a sales and marketing-minded individual like myself. The class was led by Dr. Michael L. Sesnowitz, PhD, who had decades of experience in the field. On that particular day, Dr. Sesnowitz entered the classroom and hurriedly threw his briefcase and books onto the desk and paced about the front of the room without a word. He was visibly upset. After a couple of moments, he planted himself on the top of the desk, forcibly exhaled, and said, "Listen up! I have something important to tell you!" This never happened before, so we sat up and became extremely interested in what sage wisdom might be imparted in that moment. As we perched forward in our chairs with our full attention on his next move, he looked at us earnestly and said, "When you leave here, each one of you will become a specialist in something. My advice to you is to specialize in something that is lucrative ... OK, let's get into the next chapter of your text." Mic drop.

As I sat there in stunned silence, weighing the significance of his comment, he continued on with the class as if nothing had just happened. But for me, it was the one lesson — the one moment — that made the whole MBA worth every penny. Those fifteen months of study were mostly a blur, but as it is said that life comes down to a few moments, this one was a doozy.

I knew before I attended grad school that I was going to own my own financial planning firm. It was just a field of particular interest and purpose for me. So since that time, I have become a personal finance expert and have successfully established, developed, and sold two financial planning firms, retiring at age fifty. However, retirement is not for people like me, so now I specialize in consulting on business and tax planning. Why? Because it is lucrative! Especially for my clients!

Earning a fortune, whatever that is for you, is the sum of the answers to some very important questions. I will ask these questions for the purpose of assisting you in attaining the correct answers to create the level of income you desire.

The first important question is "In what area shall I specialize?" To answer this, we must understand the meaning of a "specialist." According to the Concise Oxford English Dictionary, it is "a person who concentrates on a particular subject or activity; a person highly skilled in a specific field." Based on this definition, we can readily see these individuals in every area of endeavor in life. Just look at any professional — artist, tradesperson, athlete, technician, teacher, and so on — and you see a specialist who has made the commitment to concentrate on and become highly skilled in one primary area of activity. We find that the most skilled in our society can gain notoriety for being considered "the best" in what they do. Since we see the "highly skilled" becoming famous and the "not-so-highly skilled" becoming infamous, it should be obvious that attempting to concentrate on more than one area at a time until you are "highly skilled" is a fool's errand and will result in "questionably skilled in ambiguous fields," which neither results in competence nor recompense — the jack-of-all-trades abyss. A good example of a true specialist is Grant Cardone. He became most well-known for mastering the one subject of sales to the point that he become the largest sales trainer in the world. That was his first skill; from there, he became highly skilled in other areas to expand his influence and his empire. Having personally known and worked with him over the last several years, his commitment to excellence and focus are clearly the driving factors to his success.

While I am fortunate to have been given this advice from Dr. Sesnowitz, it is equally unfortunate that I got that advice just when I was at the end of my formal education. Way too late, in my opinion. This is something that every person needs to consider *before* they choose to train for any trade or profession. Because the truth is, society places values on every good or service in the economy, and if you choose to become a specialist in a field of "low value," then either you have to accept the compensation related to that field or become a specialist in some other "high-value" field. If your education and training are not properly directed to becoming a specialist in an area that furthers your passion and purpose and compensates you in a way that is acceptable to you, then you have essentially wasted that time and money (something high school students and their parents should understand before choosing career paths).

After we decide our specialization, we then attempt to solve the problem of no or low income by asking the following question: "How do I make more money?" While this seems to be a popular inquiry, I submit to you that it is the wrong question. Why? The universe gives us *exactly* what we ask for, so this question is not going to produce any results for two reasons. First, only central banks can make money, so if you aren't empowered with the authority to print money, then this question doesn't even apply to you. Second, the idea of "making money" is asked from the position of *effect*, giving us the idea that we are trying to receive something valuable based on the actions of some external and nebulous *cause*.

The correct question is "How do I create more value?" This is the correct question because it properly places the individual as the causative force in the equation. It places the focus on doing something as a first action, then, in the correct sequence, receiving something as a second action. It is a fascinating commentary that, in the general public, there seems to be a mystery regarding how money is earned. Most people have a vague idea that they go to a job and every couple of weeks they receive money. There really doesn't seem to be any observation that the work was performed and then the money was received, in that order. Even when getting paid in advance, the money is not earned until the result is delivered.

Specialists are experts at getting results, for that is the only thing that matters. "Highly skilled" means that you know and can use the tools and techniques of your field well enough to obtain a high-quality result that then has value in the marketplace. This result, whether a completed good or service, is then traded with the public you serve in return for other items of value: money, referrals, goodwill, and other consideration.

The amount of money you make is directly proportional to the amount of perceived value you deliver.

What is perceived value? Oxford defines "value" as "the regard that something is held to deserve; the importance, worth, or usefulness of something." And what is it that we humans consider valuable? The avoidance of pain and the attainment of pleasure. But since people will do way more to avoid pain than to gain pleasure, value could be summed up in the solving of problems. "Perceive" can be defined as "regard as" or "apparent." So in this case it may not be actual value, but will be regarded as value despite its potentially dubious effects. This is the phenomenon of vice — drugs, smoking, gambling, and so on — which is perceived as solving a problem while having deleterious effects on the consumer. When you create actual value that is then consumed by your patrons, the person and the society all benefit from improved conditions.

At this juncture, this critical question must be asked: "Am I the absolute best specialist in my field for my area of influence?" If the answer is no, then you need to do everything you can to improve your technical results. For example, if you are a dentist, review, improve, and drill your procedures until you are executing them as close to perfectly as possible. If you are a sales professional, review, improve, and drill your sales presentations, objection handlings, and prospecting techniques until you are at the level of an Olympic athlete in competence and execution.

This is the make-or-break of your income because people want to be served by the best, and if you don't *know* you're the best, then how can you promote the confidence and evidence of results needed to gain the confidence of your public? You can't. It all starts with you.

In my seminars, I would ask this question, and it shocked me how many highly competent professionals felt reserved about saying they were "the best," as though it would be somehow viewed as arrogant or boastful. But when they began to own it, their confidence shot up like a rocket and miraculously their sales went up, even while sitting there in the seminar room.

Once you have the technical side dialed in, then ask the next question: "*Whom* do I serve?" This is called your public — the group of people who are best suited to receive the greatest benefits from your goods and/or services and who can also pay you properly for your expertise. This is not everyone, but a small niche of those who you can serve better than anyone else. One great example was John, a physical therapist I counseled a few years ago. He was struggling with trying to do therapy on average people, not getting paid by insurance, and having way too much overhead. He never really zeroed in on his exact specialty or public. At a seminar, he shared with me that he had a client who rode in the Tour de France and treated an Olympic downhill skier. I pleaded with him to rebrand himself as "the premier PT exclusive to world-class athletes" and he would be in demand all over the world, make a high income with cash-paying clients and virtually eliminate his overhead. He could have created and owned the market. I don't know what became of him, but that one shift in his business mindset would have been life-changing and lucrative!

The next critical question: "How will I become the go-to expert when anyone in my public encounters the problem I specialize in solving?" You may be a rock star specialist in your field, and you may have your public well-defined, but if no one knows you exist, you'll be broke. This is the biggest problem I encounter when consulting business owners: a gross underestimation of the level of marketing needed to create the top-of-mind awareness in your public and a viable and expanding business. If you do not have more people to see than you have time and resources to see them, then your marketing needs improvement. That is the test. It is impossible to expand with new personnel and equipment if you do not have the paying customers to finance the additional overhead. Think in terms of increasing five times to ten times what you currently execute in marketing activities.

Your marketing strategy is really broken down into just a few specializations, all of which have their role to play in creating a lucrative enterprise. The first is surveys. Surveys allow you to find out from your public exactly what they value, how to offer it to them, and what they will pay for it, all by asking a series of precise questions. The second is branding, which is your unique identity and mark of quality that separates you from your competition — logos, taglines, mission statements, etc. It is successful to the degree that you can create a reputation of extraordinary quality and value. The third is content creation — communicating your expertise and delivering real value for free *before* you ask for anything in return. The fourth specialization is getting attention. This is done by getting on every possible media channel with your image and your content, as well as expanding your database and getting people to see that you exist. This, of course, is never-ending because you never know when that prospect will encounter the exact problem you can solve. But when they do, you will be there, top-of-mind. Your job is to keep communicating and delivering more and more perceived value to more and more of your target public every day. The money and other value will flow back to you.

The final question in our series is "What other goods and/or services can I provide my public that complement my current specialty?" That can be ascertained simply by assessing your current resources and asking your current clients what they will consider valuable, so that you know what to offer. The goal is to create multiple income streams by creating ancillary services that augment your current offerings, in alignment with your brand. This can create synergy and provide far greater value for your clients and income for you.

Dr. Sesnowitz would no doubt be surprised to learn of the effect his comment made on me that spring day in 1991. Even though you were not in attendance, you now have the benefit of the wisdom he conveyed. As it turns out, most any specialization can become lucrative when one also masters marketing and sales. I invite you to heed this advice and ask yourself the preceding questions, obtain workable answers, and put them into action to earn your fortune.

* ☆ ⭐ ☆ *

ABOUT CHRISTOPHER MUSIC

Christopher is a twenty-nine-year veteran of the personal financial planning profession. He has owned and sold two firms since 1992, resulting in the improvement of the financial destinies of thousands of families in the U.S. He is a best-selling author, international speaker, and podcaster on financial topics. A certified business consultant, registered financial consultant, and a certified business exit consultant, he is committed to expanding his knowledge and expertise in the fields of personal finance and economics.

After creating the industry's first scientifically based financial planning system, he has continued to innovate new services for financial advisors and small business owners with his current project, Taxnetics™, an intelligent approach to tax planning. He consults with financial professionals and business owners on many strategies to create five figures or more in yearly income tax savings.

Christopher can be reached at www.christophermusic.net and www.taxnetics.com or through his email at pchristophermusic@gmail.com.

CHAPTER 10:

A BETTER WAY FOR PHYSICIANS
(COMBATTING DEPRESSION AND SUICIDE THROUGH FINANCIAL FREEDOM)

BY GAIL L. CLIFFORD, MD, MMM, CPE, FACP, FHM

As physicians, we spend most of our lives in the left brain. It's scientific. It's factual. But it's not necessarily safe. Diagnosing and saving lives, dealing with unnecessary and preventable deaths. We think we're handling it all, balancing it all … until we're not. Physicians suffer more suicides than any profession on average, more than one each day.

Spending time in the right brain is one way to ease the burdens. But sometimes, most times, we become so engulfed by the pressure to pay off our student loans (80 percent have debt, too many with more than $300K in debt) that we can't focus on anything else.

When I came out of medical school, I had $250K in debt, mostly at an interest rate of 18–20 percent. I did everything possible to keep the interest in deferment — even going back to school, since tuition was so much cheaper than paying even the interest owed.

What I wish I'd been able to do, and what my genius zone is now, is help people learn to be OK with their debt. What if we split our resources to pay the minimum amount possible on the loan while building assets that will create passive income? Your loans can be paid at the lowest stress to you, and in the end, you'll have assets to live from.

It's a mindset shift that will rid you of the necessity of trading your time for money and let you build the life of your dreams before your retirement. Don't just work on saving enough that you can have 4 percent withdrawn each year as you scrimp in retirement. I want you to live in abundance after the early years of particularly focused work when you're building the initial assets.

When I started in private practice, there were no government subsidies. There was no help paying back loans over longer periods of time. There was no loan forgiveness. And they even took away the tax deduction on interest payments — I "just missed" whatever benefit used to exist … every time. And the government was shut down, so programs offering loan repayment didn't have the ability to accept anyone.

We scrimped and saved and put every possible penny towards student loans — just over $50K during my first year in private practice, after taxes! And my principal went *up* by $2,000! My husband and I just stared at each other, exhausted, defeated. How were we ever going to get through this? How could we ever have more children if we couldn't even pay my loans?

Sound familiar?

Then I lost him and I was on my own, supporting our daughter and needing a nanny just so I could get my job done. Any bonus, any refund, any rebate … anything that didn't need to go directly into our daily living expenses or our daughter's college fund went into the student loan repayment bucket. Living incredibly inexpensively, I slowly made progress.

At times, I'd even work two jobs — or picked up as many extra shifts as I could. Exhausting. It took twenty-three years (1987–2010) and $1.3 million to pay off my original student loans. I'm the "banker's dream," my dad always said. "They wouldn't loan you the money if they didn't think you could pay it off."

And then it was time for my daughter to go to college. I'd saved $100K for her schooling during my five years in private practice before she started first grade.

Unfortunately, with the market timing and so on, my investments hadn't grown much in those eighteen years and she chose a very expensive school — so those funds only lasted the first of her seven years in higher education. And because I didn't want our daughter to have college loans, I worked two jobs — eighty-four hours a week on average — for nearly seven years to pay the extra $187K per year (7 x $187k + 100K = $1.409 million). I know not everyone is able to do this, but I was determined not to have her face the same challenges I did — especially since she had no interest in medicine (thank God) and was unlikely to have the revenue generation possible from my profession.

WHAT IF THERE WAS A BETTER WAY?

Why can't we take the approach of Robert and Kim Kiyosaki to build the assets that will produce the passive income to pay off your school debt, your children's education, or your retirement? What would it take to do that?

I realized early on that two-physician couples were not my audience. They could live easily on one physician's income and use the other's income to pay off the debt in a small number of years. My market is the single mom or the sole breadwinner who is willing to take the extra time — to make the extra time, to carve it out of the day — to create assets that can be developed into passive income.

Spending half an hour a day, or three hours a week, you can create assets you'll invest to develop passive income that can replace your ordinary income over time and painlessly pay off your student loans.

How long does it take to get there?

It depends on how much time you put in up front.

Fortunately, many student loan programs allow longer terms to pay off loans. It's going to seem counter-intuitive, but bear with me here. If you take the longer time to pay off your student debt at low interest rates, you have lower monthly payments. If you have lower monthly payments, you can take the money you've saved and put it into income-generating assets — which are taxed to you at a much lower rate than your ordinary income.

And you can learn where it's important to spend money and where you can save.

For example, there are four places where you can lower your expenses significantly and fairly painlessly:

1. Taxes;

2. Insurance;

3. Interest;

4. Investment expenses.

By making simple fixes, you save money, which you then invest in real estate or stocks — the only two places I've found where you actually, reliably generate income. I'm *not* talking about flipping houses — though if that's something you enjoy, I salute you. That provides bolus amounts of cash you need to roll over fairly quickly to avoid taxation. This would be more along the lines of rental properties or multi-family units.

If you can avoid buying a single-family home but start by purchasing a duplex instead, for example, and rent out the other side for the cost of your mortgage? You've got my system down. For me, I earned extra income using intellectual property instead of real property — I write.

I wrote screenplays, took copywriting courses, and then finally landed in travel writing. It was an easy blend of my love of travel and love of sharing stories with people that would either entertain or make their lives easier.

Just prior to the COVID-19 pandemic, I was making enough money to pay my household bills with that writing income and hire my daughter as an employee. My physician income could finally go to building assets in retirement. And I found a few good groups of people to help me.

The old way of paying off debt involved living a small, economical life and working extra hours, extra shifts, trading your time for the money to pay off the loans faster.

The wealthy view things differently. They manage their income to invest in assets that produce passive income. That pays for their daily needs, so it's barely a thought on their radar.

It takes time, energy, sometimes even sweat and tears. But once you've put the system in place, you can spend less than thirty minutes a day. You'll experience the freedom you probably thought you needed to wait for retirement to experience.

THE BETTER WAY

I took action on my dream in 2008 and, as of 2020, I help fellow physicians learn this new way of paying off debt. When you follow my program, you can get paid around the clock. You'll receive the individualized help you need to map out the exact steps to build your million-dollar businesses.

The better way includes helping you strategize how to generate more income, yet relieve stress from your demanding career.

Think how much better you'll feel when the financial burden is lifted.

Skip time-wasting mistakes and get rid of your low-yield tasks.

Learn how to make money quickly by focusing solely on what gets you paid. And outsource the things you hate to do, even if you're good at them, so you can spend your time working on the high-yield tasks that will grow your business faster.

It's not all about earning your way to being a millionaire.

You can't earn your way to wealth or save your way to freedom. It's about enjoying the life you have now as you build your portfolio to protect yourself and your family so you can return your focus, when you want, to the practice of medicine.

This program, an online course with group and individual coaching, will work for anyone — but I focus on physicians and medical students because I'm tired of witnessing the pain I endured and see my colleagues go through today.

We need to start protecting and supporting each other. And we need to stop trying to do it on our own. That leads to deep depression or anxiety when we fail. I don't want anyone to experience that.

It's not about waiting to have enough money. It's about creating the life we've always wanted … right *now*. Stop being confused about the difference between being rich and being free.

We diligently work in the traditional ways to earn more income, pay off more debt, and try to build our retirement. Instead, let's take a break from piling our income towards the debt and invest as much as humanly possible early, when we have the advantage of the time value of money, to grow our investments.

Put off those low-interest student loans as much as you can.

Seriously, if you can build an asset that will pay off a $1,000 loan each month, the loan will be paid off eventually, and you'll be left with a revenue-generating asset.

How can you say no to that?

Unless you're not willing to put in the work. I get that. If so, this program is not for you. That's okay.

I want you to be fulfilled in every part of your life — physical, mental, emotional, spiritual, and financial. However you get there is great.

But understanding the financial pieces and solving them in a way that benefits you in the long term has become my genius zone.

And taking action is a must. Ultimately, analysis and discussion serve towards achieving a tangible result. But don't get bogged down in analysis paralysis. I'll connect you to the right people, as I have with hundreds of clinicians, to better balance life and work.

Issues faced by our colleagues often parallel your situation, so the advice I gave that person, and how things turned out, could apply to you. Mostly, this advice is about navigating your professional life, but I'm also happy to share wisdom about parenting, money, and keeping life exciting.

I am not a financial planner and want you to get your own legal and financial advice. But I've been through this, twice, to the tune of $1.3 million+ both times, and have learned some of the easier, better ways for you to get there.

I want you to have the money you want to live the life you want. I want you to be able to get up each day and *want* to go to work and help patients live their best lives and heal quickly.

I want you to want this for yourself. But during this pandemic, so many of us don't want to go into work at all — or worse, can't.

REDUCE THE PRESSURE

How many physicians take their own lives rather than find a different path? I recall a hero ER physician in New York City, Dr. Lorna Breen, who treated patients and then contracted COVID-19, survived it after a difficult battle, and went back to work — then committed suicide.

I totally get her. I'm incredibly sad for her and her family. After everything she'd witnessed, and everything she'd experienced as a well-cared-for patient receiving the best treatment available, she remained despondent.

I do not know her, and may be guessing, but having experienced that profound depression on my side, I can imagine that being placed in a position to allot scarce resources could have been one of the factors that led to her committing suicide.

I'd like to stop that from happening. I want physicians to get financially free as soon as possible so that, when we are discouraged, we can pause, take a sabbatical, do something else, or even retire.

Financial stress is the second-worst pressure most physicians face.

Let's free ourselves from that. Close the financial books on medical school.

My goal and your mission, should you choose to accept it, is to reduce that pressure and increase the joy in your life. Get your system in place and spend thirty minutes a day or three hours a week to allow yourself true financial freedom.

At the very least, you'll be able to just walk away from medicine, if that's what you need to do.

Value and spend time in your right brain. The life you save may be your own.

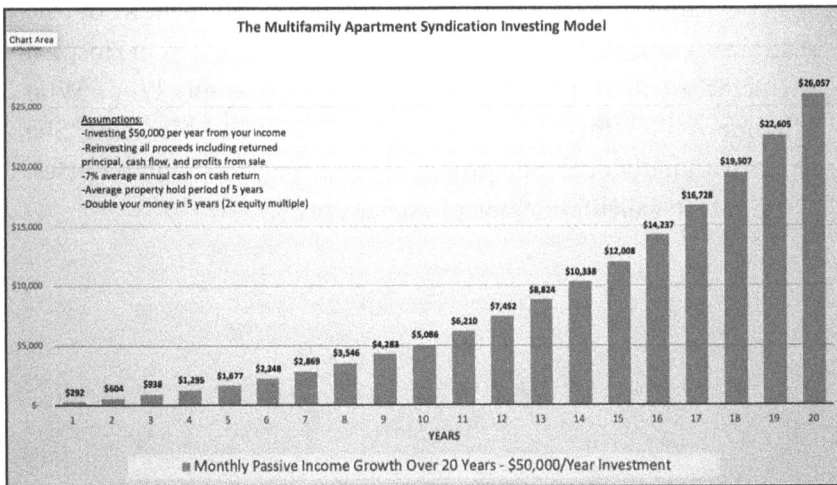

The Multifamily Apartment Syndication Investing Model

Chart Area

Assumptions:
- Investing $50,000 per year from your income
- Reinvesting all proceeds including returned principal, cash flow, and profits from sale
- 7% average annual cash on cash return
- Average property hold period of 5 years
- Double your money in 5 years (2x equity multiple)

Values by year: $292, $604, $938, $1,295, $1,677, $2,348, $2,869, $3,546, $4,283, $5,086, $6,210, $7,452, $8,824, $10,338, $12,008, $14,237, $16,728, $19,507, $22,605, $26,057

YEARS

■ Monthly Passive Income Growth Over 20 Years - $50,000/Year Investment

About Gail Clifford

Dr Gail Clifford is a board-certified Internal Medicine hospitalist and international best-selling author. A professor since 1996, she's been teaching residents, students, and junior colleagues how to better balance life-work ratios and create wealth to pay off debt in a better way. Ultimately, her goal is to reduce physician stress and, subsequently, the frequency of physician suicide, by creating passive assets to pay student, or any, debt so you can stop trading time for paychecks and embrace the joy of medicine that led you to pursue the path in your youth.

If you want someone to help you make tough choices about what you want to accomplish and establish concrete goals with timelines and milestones, she is the mentor for you. She's solution-oriented and eschews the status quo (we can do better!). Be forewarned: she has a strong bias toward action.

Dr. Clifford is a professional member and Fellow of the American College of Physicians and Fellow of the Society of Hospital Medicine. In 2018, Dr. Clifford received the Marquis Who's Who Lifetime Achievement Award for Contributions to Medicine. She works with individuals and groups via coaching and online courses.

Contact: gailclifford@ablephysicians.org

CHAPTER 11:

THE "D" STANDS FOR "DIFFERENCE"
(DEDICATING A SECOND CHANCE AT LIFE TO
IMPROVING THE LIVES OF OTHERS)

BY PETER MAGANA

My life has been very challenging. In the end, I'm thankful and I'm humbled.

In 1980, as a D student, I dropped out of high school in my senior year. I was also a little ADHD, but I felt like I had the mindset of an A student. Today, that D is making a Difference in people's lives, and that A is taking Action to succeed in life.

I got married at a young age and had two children, and I had a stable job to support my family. I started doing labor work at a paint industry and worked my way up to senior tech. At twenty-two years old, I was a typical renter. I was just living life, you know, not thinking about owning a home or anything like that. An opportunity naturally emerged when a co-worker was having trouble selling his home. He approached me and asked if I was interested in taking it over. I replied, "Okay, what do I do?"

He said, "Well, just take over the payments and I'll grant it to you, and then I'll give it to you."

I said, "Oh my God, really, that's it? Sold!" I was a little nervous about this. Still, I was excited. I really didn't know much about real estate, but it provided an opportunity to have $100 more a month as I would be paying less than I had been on rent. My wife and I were raising our children, so this was a welcome situation. The house did have a $10,000 equity, which I gladly accepted.

Of course, I had a Plan B in place in case the property didn't work out: I would just go ahead and sell it (or whatever, you know). The main thought that came to my mind was moving forward 100 percent. That was my big start as a homeowner. My goodness, I found it incredibly interesting that I — a person without much money or credit to speak of — would be able to obtain a home. This decision would later become a major inspiration behind my message of homeownership. Without any clue as to the inner workings of real estate, I took a shot, and it ended up being the best life-changing event, period.

I was told by my coworker a year later that I would need to put the property under my name. Of course, I thought that was already the case. It wasn't yet, so I had the deed put in my name. Beyond the property, he also wanted me to take his home loan under my name as well, which would get him out of that completely. I was figuring out how these things would work out as I went through that process.

When I filled out the application under FHA, my credit was not good. This meant that I needed to fix it or it would be difficult to get a loan, and I had no money down. I needed to figure out how to structure this transaction. My credit was affected by a repossession at an earlier stage of my life. I was a young man hindered by old history. I told the lender that it was incorrect information; it was too stagnant. Because the repossession was old, I was able to negotiate with them, and they actually removed the item from my records. Therefore, because it was erased, I was able to get that portion taken care of for the approvals process.

As I needed a loan, I made a plan to gift myself some money in order to make it look like a down payment. We actually made this transaction as a purchase, and we acquired the property for $73,000. Lo and behold, I did get the $10,000 because there was equity in the property. The seller signed it over to me.

This required creativity, talent, and an acceptance that there's a possibility to acquire anything. It just takes a little time to work out the process. I found myself wanting to learn more. At that age of twenty-three, I decided to change my life and leave my current occupation. Further down the road, from my experience with figuring out how to make things work, I was able to overcome the most difficult situations in anybody's files: credit issues, bill collections, structuring transactions, applying more money, understanding the market, up-trending and down-trending (buyer's or seller's) markets, and so forth. Yes, it took a lot of talent and many years to master the process, but I soon realized that…

ANYTHING IS POSSIBLE!

As far as I'm concerned, 90 percent of clients I work with have some kind of issue; but we're able to overcome and resolve this, and then secure a home. As long as they stick with the program as I guide them through it, we can secure the outcome. It surely takes confidence, time, and building up their level of trust, but we can secure and handle each and every transaction opportunity.

Most people today are spending more on rent than an actual mortgage. I believe that the main problem here is that most of them never look into the reality of it, or how the ownership process works. I can empathize with that. I was in the same situation with my first home. I never thought I would be a homeowner, and I had no understanding of the process. Still, I took the opportunity, and I was able to get through it. As far as I'm concerned, as I tell my clients, the most important part is taking action.

Later in my life, I partnered with broker/lender Naomi Cox for assistance in finance. I was able to work with Naomi to open a real estate company and we grew from there to a small office, and we did well. I also learned by watching TV programs on flips and going to free flip seminars to learn. I built up my confidence and knew I had to take calculated risks, so I took action and started an investment company and started to flip homes without using any of my money, meaning I was using other people's money (OPM). I became a good negotiator — I got every property that I wanted from sellers with fixer-uppers, and 100 percent making a deal as a win-win situation — and the key to all that was just being honest.

Because of working many years in the paint industry, I had developed a liver disease, and I became ill in 2008. I was in need of a liver transplant. It wasn't until August 28th, 2014, that I received one. I suffered dearly during those six years. My daughter became my living donor, meaning she provided 65 percent of her liver for me to survive. She is literally the only reason why I'm here.

I'm thankful and blessed for my amazing daughter's decision, and my faith in God. When I fully recovered, I found myself filled with a new passion for life. While I had mastered the home purchasing process, I had not yet taken it to the next level. For myself, I had a home that was worth over a million dollars. While I was sick, I knew that if I died, everything would be taken care of. I didn't have life insurance, but I did have enough money. My house was very important, so I know the importance of homeownership.

Let me tell you, when you're on your deathbed, you realize that life is more beautiful than anything; it all becomes so much more serious. Life is more precious than what we could possibly imagine, and that became very clear to me. I think that we all tend to overthink things. I want to help others build beyond that and take action. Time is of the essence, as it is with many things. Too often, people trap themselves in the ever-looping cycle of paying rent, and they're throwing their money away when they could actually acquire a home instead.

Due to my clear understanding about how precious time can be, I was inspired toward the concept of creating a quick approach to homeownership. I wanted to help others beat the negative thought that there wasn't enough time or energy to get this done quickly. So we shortened the process in the hopes of creating an opportunity for action.

My life mission is to inspire and motivate people with a take-action approach. My passion is giving back to the world and giving all that I have to my daughter. She motivated me to see things in a different way. She sacrificed part of her life, so I want to sacrifice part of mine and give to the world to improve the future.

I was told that I was at risk for the first year after my surgery. The doctor said that if anything were to go wrong, organ rejections would happen within that time frame. I was blessed and had no side effects. I was well. So, in 2015, I took action toward my dreams and studied to get my broker's license in order to make the impact as I had envisioned it.

I'll tell you straight, I failed that test miserably. In fact, I failed it twenty-six times in total. I passed on the twenty-seventh test. I went through so many emotions over the course of the real estate exams. Right back to that ADHD brain, I kept thinking I was totally dumb. I reached a moment where I was so close, with seventy-four points, but I needed seventy-five. It felt like the government didn't want me to pass. I had family telling me that maybe this wasn't the direction for me. No. I didn't care. I never quit. So I tell people today that I studied twenty-six times, retriggering my brain to study differently for the ultimate and final test. I passed. Let me tell you, if something doesn't work, keep changing, and you will have a different outcome.

Living by My Motto

After I earned my license, I wanted to start a company where a man and woman could create a business together. Well, women's intelligence was added to men's strength in February of 2016 when I met Milagro Abeyta. She was kind and professional and was helping seniors in her line of work. She really cared and worked long hours at times with no pay.

We spent the next four years facing challenges. Through those, we created the American Dream Yes We Can (ADYWC) movement, helping people see a clear and simple path to homeownership. To my surprise, we became a nonprofit in 2020. Working with powerful women leaders, we took a concept that was attracting the consumers to our "motivate, inspire, and take action" approach. We found ourselves uniting real estate agents, lenders, credit repair companies, and vendors. We held them all accountable and we became the voice of the consumer as we built trust, advocating for them and guiding them to the American dream. We still host virtual events, and look forward to returning to live events.

From this experience, to the end of my days, my motto is transparency, accountability, and trust. The ADYWC experience led to my second company, Renovation Listing Agent. We help homeowners sell their property when it needs work and they can't afford it or they need to sell for less than the value. We help fix and improve what is needed to sell, with no upfront cost to the homeowner, and we get reimbursed at close of escrow. We also partner with sellers who have major fixer-uppers or people that inherit a property that needs a lot of work. What we do to help is set a guaranteed set price as is. We rehab the property to sell at maximum value, and then we split the net profit by adding more money in addition to their already set net profit. It's a win-win approach.

EL SUEÑO AMERICANO
THE AMERICAN DREAM

All of this culminated into a third company called the D-Billionaire Club. In early 2021, we will invite one million people to join. Back in December of 2019, I told myself that I would die someday. And I made myself think about the question: if I had a billion dollars, what would I do with it? My answer was that I wanted to help people by assisting in financing flip homes as well as having celebrity guest speakers to inspire and motivate and teach. And, for anyone with an idea or invention or world-changing concept that could help impact people's lives, we would support them by funding their invention and helping with manufacturing. Overall, we would only take 10 percent to put it back into the pot.

My vision for D-Billionaire Club will make history: to be on the books by raising $1 billion in less than six months. I invite you to take part. We have over sixty million Latinos as our core audience, and the club is open to anyone. Imagine the benefit of having a tribe of one million people, and access to funds and life-changing concepts.

BEYOND 2020: ANYTHING IS STILL POSSIBLE!

Over the course of such a dark start for a new decade, my partners and I continued reinventing ourselves in the most positive way. By working together through these challenging times, there is greatness and opportunity with the right mindset and unity to help each other. The American dream is still possible. And when it comes to moving forward, there is only one reply: Yes, we can.

If you'd like to see what we're up to today, please visit theamerican-dreammovement.com. And if you want to join the newest movement, I welcome you to the D-Billionaire Club at dbillionaireclub.com.

I have a new life, and I will do everything in my power to ensure that it's the best. I encourage you not to wait for loss or emergencies to seize your future. You don't need a second chance to take action. But if you do need it, starting in 2021, I think you're already living it.

ABOUT PETER MAGANA

Peter Magana lives a life of gratitude. He thanks his daughter, Yvonne Magana, for saving his life by providing 65 percent of her liver. He thanks God for blessing him with such a beautiful family.

Beyond a second chance at life, Peter aims to help others and change lives, and he strives to motivate people to see their own potential, and to both inspire and educate them in building confidence, living their dreams, and accomplishing their goals by taking action.

An infinite source of positivity, Peter feels that anything and all things are possible. Through his work, he shares this belief while fulfilling his purpose to make the world a better place, one life at a time.

Over the course of five years after receiving surgery, Peter worked hard toward bringing his vision to reality. His work in the real estate industry has resulted in many people accomplishing the American dream of homeownership! Such endeavors have led to further opportunities for Peter and his team to make a difference.

CHAPTER 12:

NO PERMISSION
(THREE STEPS TO HAPPINESS BY DESIGN)

BY HELENA T. JUNG

Have you wondered whether the 2020-2021 pandemic has changed who we are? Research shows that it has amplified the way we burn ourselves down and out as a society. And it has revealed a special opportunity, too. With everybody just having been locked up at home, a majority of people and families now have some serious lack of happiness to work on. Don't we?

This has impacted mothers in a special way. Most moms didn't sign up for what they are getting. Nobody seems to really know what they signed up for either. It's just common sense that it doesn't have to be fun or easy. "Being Mom" became one of the highest imaginable standards a long time ago. It has become a duty to the point where many mothers feel like they cannot juggle another one of those heavy curveballs life keeps throwing these days.

How can that be cured?

For society, families, and especially for partners observing the symptoms, the right answer seems out of reach.

There is a better way.

But before we talk about that, let me share a story with you.

"ENOUGH!"

I remember the first call with one wonderful soul like it happened this morning.

Lia was in her mid-thirties. She looked concerned. Her body was signaling tension. Apart from that, she was remarkably neat, smiling. She looked into her smartphone camera like a professional TV anchor and jumped straight to the point: "Helena, it has happened … can I have your ear for five minutes?"

Lia shared her story with me. How she felt that she was taken for granted. How she felt stretched.

I remember Lia so well, not because her situation was unique. Quite the opposite. Most of the mothers I worked with during the COVID-19 lockdowns felt a deep crisis of energy and meaning, either already at full swing or closing in on them. Most of them felt overly relied on by politicians, bosses, teachers, family … and themselves.

Lia was different in a very fresh and adorable way. She had an unconventionally clear perspective on family and her role in it. And she thought she had found that cure that could set herself and her family free in one of our trainings.

Lia looked at me with an excited expression on her face. "I really want that to work. And I understand I have to renegotiate the deal here first..." Then she took on a presidential pose, put on her Sunday smile, and spelled out a declaration:

"I hereby resign from my role as the mother!"

What followed over the course of the next few weeks should go down in the culture of a soon-to-be #wondermoms tribe.

BURNING MOM

Lia had spent magical first afternoon at home with her newborn son, Tom, on a clear, sunny, winter day five years prior to our phone call. Tom was fast asleep most of the time and a happy kid those other times. She enjoyed every second of her new role.

For Lia, filling this new role as a mother would bring endless joy. It would also change the fabric of her reality. It would impact her relationship with her partner, with her career, with money — and most importantly, it had already started impacting her relationship with herself.

Over the course of the next five years, Lia and Tom's dad, Michael, would share the most adorable moments. A trance-like dream that didn't want to end.

With Michael returning to his pre-family work schedule and Tom growing, Lia's days got busier. Feeding, washing, walking, putting Tom to sleep, cramming a phone call with her best friend into the calendar, waking Tom, feeding, washing, cooking for Michael and herself, and sitting at a beautiful table at the end of the day, Lia found herself tired and increasingly feeling empty.

Two years after Tom arrived, Sofia was born. Lia was still 100 percent committed to doing the best job any mom could do. More importantly, Lia felt she had to make the experience fun for everybody.

She took pride in and gratitude from getting the kids to kindergarten with cozy, fresh clothes and a healthy "breakfast to go" that would let the small souls feel her love in every inch of their little bodies. Happy for her new part-time job, she would then turn to the tiny and silent home-office space that she had built and start organizing projects for a marketing agency for at least a few hours.

In this Instagram world of seeming perfection, it can be very easy to feel defective and behind. Lia sometimes got an intense feeling of exclusion from this kaleidoscope of exceptional mothers blending into one prototype of everything she felt she was not: those cooking top-managers with multilingual kids, sharing their newest protein cakes from an outsized shiny new kitchen, looking like a cover girl from a fitness magazine in skinny jeans that looked more expensive than her car.

Lia felt like she couldn't get enough things done. And she couldn't get them done well enough. So, she stretched more…

And instead of picturing herself behind a closed bathroom door, carrying a sign that read "Keep out. Happy and caring mom in the making ☺," Lia started to wonder: "What the hell is wrong with me?"

MOMENTS OF TRUTH

Three months before our phone call, Lia found herself obsessing over self-optimization. Wondering "what's wrong with me?" had self-inflated into certainty. She was convinced she was broken. And she was determined to find a fix.

Interestingly, one of the pit stops she identified (in addition to thyroid detox, HIIT training routines, and some nutritional kung-fu) was an "anti-burnout" online training course that she attended. And one thought from this event got stuck in her mind.

It was the simple idea that maybe her battery worked just the way everybody else's battery worked.

That being a mother didn't guarantee endless energy. This thought started to grow, and Lia started seeing the energy she poured into all those little day-to-day tasks.

"DOES THAT REALLY HAVE TO BE MY LIFE?"

Slowly, it started to make sense. She was finding herself in an energy-drained and endlessly tiring spot, but because she was a defect. Not because she needed to be fixed. She got to this point because she didn't treat herself right. In order to light up other people's lives and spread some warmth, Lia was burning herself out and into the ground. And she had seen many other strong mothers do the same.

A few days later, there was a moment of absolute clarity. Lia understood very quickly that it would not make sense to beat herself or anybody else up for being in that bad place. She wanted that to change. Her main question evolved into "What am I waiting for?"

So she made the decision to do something about it. And it started with understanding this:

If she could give away control over her life, she could also claim it back. Nobody owned her and she didn't need any permission.

Lia had made a decision that would improve the quality of her own life as well as those around her as well as their relationships, fulfillment, and even their impact on the world.

How? Well ... it only took three things.

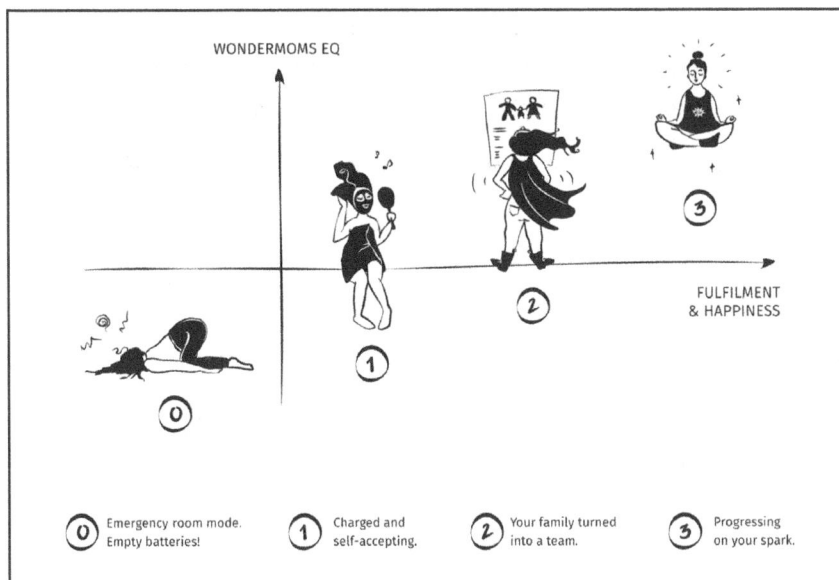

WONDERMOM STEPS

Lia's struggles with the "mom" identity, her ultra-high standards, and a grown-up energy crisis are not the exception. Would you agree?

More and more mothers feel overwhelmed and unfulfilled and question their competence.

The truth, as we see it, is that moms rock.

Mothers can easily be viewed as the root and cause of good in this world and the source of almost everything in a multitude of ways. They are not broken, they don't need to be fixed, and they have every right to a wonderful life on their terms.

Here are the three steps — and one prerequisite — that have helped Lia and many others go from struggle and trying to fix themselves to building a dream life with their families.

Prerequisite

Although this is not a step, it is the most important and arguably the hardest part. If we want to take our lives to that next level, we have to make it a certainty. And a good way to get over that fence and make a decision is by using these two thoughts.

1. We need to understand what happens if nothing changes. Then visualize that and deeply feel the adversity and pain. Can you allow that?

2. We're talking about you. Ask yourself: who owns you? You don't look like you need to wait for permission or grades. You are already a miracle to most people around you. Can you claim your life?

Step 1: Go from Drain to Fill

When we have an unromantic look at your very own energy, we understand that there are two sides to it. Let's call them the "I CAN" and the "I MUST" pillars. At some point in our lives, the MUST pillar can outgrow the CAN pillar.

The tasks and responsibilities can become greater than our self-perceived competence. That's when we fall over and start feeling deeply overwhelmed and begin to burn down.

The most important ingredient: do more of what makes you happy by doing less of what just eats energy. Manage yourself as a resource. Charge.

Now that may sound easier said than done, especially on the rejection side. And that is you being unfair to yourself. Do just one thing: every time someone else tries to add to your MUST pillar, run a simple check. There is a chance that you are handling false alarms.

Instead of saying "no," try to say "I would love to…! It's difficult right now. Let's talk tomorrow."

Step 2: Turn Your Family into a Team

Sports teams experience progress together. They lead without authority. And they don't have one girl running all over the court alone in defense and offense while trying to make a five-star breakfast for the rest of the team. It's fascinating. Isn't it?

In a sports team, you don't want to work your ass off alone so that everybody else can indulge in that millionaire lifestyle. Then why do it at home?

As the new team captain in your family, you can challenge and pass things on.

Here's the most important ingredient: you want to visualize everybody's contribution to the game, including your own. Some mothers do that in the form of a poster with stickers in the kitchen. Some do it during a family reflection and share rounds of praise for each other during breakfast on Saturday. Some use a "done" list they revisit, allowing them to participate and to be rewarded with smileys, points, extra quality time, or any sort of meaningful incentive.

Step 3: Happiness by Design

What would you say if those two steps made you feel filled with positive, creative energy?

Any progress you are creating will lead to happiness. For our purposes, this goes two ways.

1. Keep up the good work in the team and celebrate progress.

2. When you think of the old times, does a hobby come to your mind? Something you really loved? Or something that other people noticed and came to you for advice on? Can you imagine blocking time just for that?

Immerse yourself in that passion. You may find it extremely rewarding not only for yourself; for many moms, that special gift turns into an income.

THE NEW LIA

Lia had that one former hobby, a real passion — something she enjoyed so deeply, she always wanted to become really good at it: baking cakes with her mom. And she especially loved them with a ton of chocolate.

With her family providing serious support and backup, Lia managed to bring her MUST pillar under control. And she noticed a change: she felt extra fun, extra energy, and extra desire. That brought her to burn some time and budget on her cake passion.

Lia's active lifestyle and the two kids motivated her to adapt the recipes to healthier versions. Some were made without sugar. Some were even completely raw. The results were astonishing and created so much extra purpose and extra passion for Lia, and her family, that the word spread quickly. Her neighbors, other mothers, and Michael's company started pre-ordering weeks of production. And before they knew it, a small new business had started to grow.

Now, every Friday afternoon, when Lia turns off her laptop to end the chat with her wondermoms circle, she goes for a run with her husband and the kids. And because her new level of self-care makes her feel accomplished and worthy, she proudly wears her new favorite shirt.

The shirt reads "I am #wondermom."

MORAL: YOU ~~CAN'T~~ WON'T HAVE IT ALL, AND THAT IS WONDERFUL

Lia's story is one of the unexpected successes that become possible when we have the courage to make room for ourselves and give ourselves permission to truly live. Even if that means the sacrifice of some minor ideals and standards. And especially when it means taking down the walls around a perfectionist self-image.

My final question for you: Can you find that spark in you?

Can you see yourself growing it? If so, then I want you to grow that inner spark so much that your neighbors will get sunburned. Become wondermom.

If you are interested in learning more about:

- How to practically turn these ideas into impact,
- How to actually do the things you understand you should do,
- How to connect with this wondermoms tribe,

I have a special, special opportunity for you!

Get your copy of an exclusive fourteen-day rescue pack for moms here: hjung.co/rescue.

ABOUT HELENA T. JUNG

It was only after a series of dramatically adverse events that, in her mid-twenties, Helena became a new entrepreneur and mother. She was convinced that, with discipline and a positive attitude, every endeavor can succeed — in professional arts, family, academia, and even business.

Later, living in a foreign country, Helena found herself with a broken marriage, looking at a pile of broken expectations that was meant to become a life, completely disillusioned and shaken. Up to that point in her biography, she had already given up her life dream of becoming a prima ballerina at the world-famous Bolshoi Theater after a twelve-year professional career in Moscow. She had moved on to study international management in Strasbourg.

When the surprisingly early death of both her parents threw her off track again, she had to jump into cold water. Balancing her parents' departure within an already overwhelming life equation required an overwhelming amount of courage and stamina. Getting out of those challenging times has helped her shape a charmingly clear nine-step process to free yourself and get rid of imaginary cages.

Helena shares her energy with a fast-growing tribe of fellow #wondermoms.

CHAPTER 13:

THE HARVEST OF THE SEED

BY REV. VICTOR ALLEN

Well, to start by saying "hello" is probably a late idea, I'm thinking, but by now you have heard that there are many different ways to skin a cat. That is just my East Texas way of saying things. Let's look at this situation from another angle. I mean, we have learned that a circle has 360 degrees. Why would we look at everything the same way, or from only one angle?

What in particular am I talking about? Success — it's at the top of everyone's agenda these days. We have some things or strategies in place to get us there. For instance, if we want to lose weight, we might buy a fitness magazine and find a diet to follow. There would then be a strategy in place to find success in weight management in our life.

One other way is by mentorship in our career field. If you want to find success in the career field of your choice, then you would then find a leader in your industry. There may be some classes that can give you the competitive advantage. These could be found at a community college or university that may offer continuing education classes.

There might be corporate trainers in your company who are willing to guide you in the right direction.

You may even find yourself at an event that expands your network. This is a great way to become successful today. Success comes as you apply yourself to the problem. As you move closer to the goal, you all of a sudden have become the solution to the problem. As you continue to educate yourself, learn new principles, and apply the real-life examples to the questions, you have now made the transition to being what is called an "expert."

Now we are evolving to the entrepreneur cure, meaning there have been some things you tried that didn't work. The information learned from the trail was needed to become successful. Today, that same information is used as a foundation to start in a positive direction.

The entrepreneur cure has to be determined to give birth to an idea that will be revolutionary to a generation. The entrepreneur cure has to be focused on success at all costs. The entrepreneur cure has to be a leader in thought patterns.

I would like to give you a closer look at my personal business and goals in life. I feel that the success of your business first depends on how you are structured. You can find many key tips in my book titled *Discover the Secrets and Power of Business Credit,* or you could simply download the e-book at www.revvictorallen.com. Be sure to take a little time to watch the video as well.

Being a man of God, I have based my study upon a biblical principle called "seedtime and harvest." This principle was taken from the first book of the Bible, when God put the finance systems in effect. This can be found in Genesis 8:22. This is God's covenant with Creation. Verse 22 says: "While the earth remains, seedtime and harvest, cold and heat, summer and winter, day and night, shall not cease."

Now, this took some time for me to try to learn and understand what all this meant to me. I thought it was very nice of God to use some things that I did understand to teach me what I didn't understand. First, "while the earth remains." Well, we are still here on Earth, so God's rules apply to us. The next one is "seedtime and harvest." This is what took time for me to understand. If I plant an apple seed, then an apple tree must grow. I had to just trust the process. To then help me and anyone else understand the order of the process, the next two statements bring in the revolutionary understanding. God then uses what I do understand: the seasons of the years and the sequence of time.

So from there, it gave me confidence that the harvest of the seed would come in the same manner. In other words, I never have to worry if day will come or if it's nighttime. I have experienced that my entire life. I never have to worry about the seasons of the year as well. They always come automatically. So I learned this in business as well, with investments.

In today's economy, the large companies are using the same seedtime and harvest principle. They are called mergers and acquisitions, or M&A. The senior management study the balance sheet of a well-run company, and then they sow a financial seed to buy the company and then reap the harvest.

I have taken this a step further in my personal business, in which I mention ways to secure funding in my book *Discover the Secrets and Power of Business Credit*.

My personal focus or my competitive advantage is that I leverage my business funding with MLPs, or master limited partnerships. MLPs have a tax advantage — they don't pay corporate taxes, which allows them to be able to pay out about 90 percent of their cash to the unit holders or partners of the business. This is a way to invest business funding at a low risk while receiving tax-free returns on capital that was invested. The quarterly distributions can then be used as the operations budget for the primary business. It can also be used to reinvest and make the quarterly checks increase.

Now this is an asset management method I use for my company. It takes some skills, research, and also the ability to understand the industry you're in. I have been in the oil and gas industry for over twenty-five years, so I'm very comfortable with the direction it's headed. And finally, America has energy independence. This is the best time in history to be involved. So my suggestion is to get in and build a position and reap the long-term rewards of the natural resources of this country.

In summary, my goal was to help someone see things from a different angle. My object was to try to help someone bridge the gap between ambition and destiny. I feel that the bridge is wisdom and knowledge, paving the road to success. My prayer is that hopefully something I said or something you read in one of the other chapters will be the bridge that you need to carry on to your God-given destiny. In the name of Jesus, amen.

ABOUT VICTOR ALLEN

The Rev. Victor Allen is a graduate of Kaplan University. He has an associate degree in information technology and is also a United States Coast Guard licensed captain. Rev. Allen has worked in the marine industry for twenty years and is a business owner of Allen Revenue Solutions, LLC. Rev. Allen also works for the City of Beaumont Police Clergy Department. He was ordained at his home church, Victory to Victory Church, in Beaumont, Texas.

The overall goal for writing this book isn't about the author. The book was composed to bridge the gap between ambition and destiny. Someone who has ambition may have gotten to a point in their life where debt stops them from reaching their destiny.

Rev. Allen mentioned a few accomplishments in the beginning; he just failed to list the duration of time to reach the goals. Sometimes our finances and resources may be out, but the drive must continue.

Who is going to teach you the financial literacy you need to bridge the gap? Yes, bridge the gap between college graduation with all the debt associated with your social security number. But you have a well-thought-out plan to launch your career. You have all the latest skills to make the plan work, but no one to fund the start-up of the operation.

Hopefully this book will give you the inside edge — the professional knowledge to launch you into your destiny. My goal is to help everyone be successful.

CHAPTER 14:

BE A PLAYMAKER

BY JEFF ROGERS

I was about to walk onstage with Stephen Colbert and Amy Sedaris as an understudy for Steve Carell at the world-renowned Second City theater in Chicago. For the uninitiated, The Second City is one of the foremost training grounds for the top comedic minds of the last sixty years, including such comedic luminaries as John Belushi, Bill Murray, Gilda Radner, Tina Fey, Amy Poehler, Chris Farley, John Candy, Eugene Levy, Dan Ackroyd, Shelley Long, George Wendt, Matt Walsh, and the list goes on and on.

Just a few years prior, I had dropped out of college and was working high-rise construction with convicts and rough men who worked hard and lived even harder. I was a union laborer and thought my life was over before it really began.

No education, no prospects, and nothing to look forward to but "a union card and a wedding coat," as Springsteen sang about on his album *The River*.

Then something magical happened. I tried to make some people laugh. Stand-up comedy was big and I thought I would give it a shot. I wasn't great, but I got some laughs, and one of the other comedians said that I should take some improv classes. She said I would learn how to be funny, but more importantly, I would learn how to be better at being myself.

It would turn out to be the best advice I ever received.

I signed up at The Players Workshop of Second City, the school for would-be improvisers. A year and a half later, I was hired by Second City for their touring company. Six months after that, I was backstage with two comedic geniuses who would go on to great fame (Colbert and Sedaris) and understudying one of the biggest comedy stars of our time (Carell).

Over the course of the next twenty years, I would win dozens of awards for creativity, innovation, and executive producing my own television show. Even stranger than that, I was being sought out by CEOs and presidents of companies, teaching them and their teams the exact system I had learned to be an agile, creative problem solver. How to be instantly innovative. How to use play as a life skill to succeed.

What made all of this possible? Improvisation. And I'm about to tell you how you can use these same tools to enjoy what you're doing. Do it with more energy and use these skills to create a life worth living. Just like I did.

Sound good? Let's play!

Let's begin with a question: ever wonder why some people succeed and others get stuck when it comes to a challenging situation? Sociologists and business scholars have a bunch of names for this ability, like blue ocean thinking (pretty, isn't it?), innovation (wow), outside the box (sounds adventurous), storytelling (very popular now), design thinking (not the decorating kind), and so on.

What they're really talking about is creativity. Creative people have the ability to look at problems and challenges differently so that they are able to overcome issues to achieve their goals. It's called a growth mindset, which is a fancy way of saying you are capable of learning. (Hint: If you're reading this right now, then you can learn. Yay, you!)

Here's the secret that nobody wants you to know: you are already a creativity super-computer!

It's true. We are born with innate creativity handed down through countless generations. It helped us survive when we lived in caves, and it's still there in the back of our brains! We just need to dust it off and plug it back in.

The question is, how do you tap into your creativity super-computer? How can you be creative on demand? And how can you share your creativity with others and lift the whole team to new creative heights?

The answer is improvisation!

Improvisation is an amazing tool for instantly tapping into creativity. Improv is used onstage at Second City and on TV in shows like *Whose Line Is It Anyway*, where players use improvisation to create scenes, plays, and entire universes right on the spot without anything but a suggestion from the audience. But improvisation is actually much more than just a tool for entertainment.

Improvisation is being taught as a critical leadership tool in universities and MBA programs from Harvard to Stanford and everywhere in between. Corporations use the simple rules of improvisation to build stronger teams and "develop agile and innovative" solutions in a fraction of the time. Similar courses are being taught at organizations such as Google, PepsiCo, MetLife, P&G, Farmer's, Otsuka, Cisco, Blue Cross Blue Shield, Motorola, and McKinsey & Company to help them become agile and open to solutions, no matter where they originate.

Now you can use the same simple lessons to become a trusted leader, sought-after ally, and creative powerhouse. Below are the basic rules for improvisation that you can use every day to build instant rapport, think faster on your feet, and tap into your brilliant creative side.

BE A PLAYMAKER

Individuals and organizations best equipped to face today's world are those that embrace uncertainty by finding creative solutions through agility, collaboration, and achieving shared goals. Companies looking to "do more with less" must get creative. So learn to be a playmaker and unleash the creative powerhouse lurking in your most important resource: your team!

Playmakers are in a constant state of calm readiness. Just like a baseball player who's standing on the balls of their feet, waiting to see where the ball will be hit — ready to go right, left, forward, or backward depending on where the ball goes. A playmaker is ready to tap into their experiences and knowledge on diverse topics at a moment's notice while connecting disparate thoughts to create breakthrough solutions.

First, you have to be open to playing. No one is talking about the "goofing off" kind of play. Instead, we think of PLAY as an acronym:

- **P is for Passion.** Let your passion be the energy that drives you to try new things and think of new ideas. (Example: Tom's Shoes.)

- **L is for Listening to Understand.** This helps you build empathy for others and see issues from multiple perspectives. (Example: Away Luggage.)

- **A is for Adaptation.** Being flexible and agile is critical for reacting and responding immediately. (Example: Best Buy.)

- **Y is for "Yes, and . . ."** More on this one next! (Example: Zappos.)

A playmaker is always asking "Why not?" They know there's more than one way to solve a problem. They think of a brainstorming session like a laboratory or sandbox where they can take problems apart and look at them from all angles to create new solutions, because you never know where the best idea will bubble up from.

THE ANSWER IS ALWAYS "YES, AND . . ."

Saying "no" is a limiting and judgmental way to block creativity. Try "yes, and . . ." instead. By agreeing with a person's idea, you validate that they have worth. The "and" allows you to add to their idea by heightening it or giving it more context.

Remember, "yes, and . . ." is not being a yes-person. You can say no with a "yes, and . . ." too. As in, "Yes, I would like dessert *and* I want to look good in my swimsuit, so I'll choose to enjoy some dessert much later ... like in the fall!"

(Also, avoid "Yes, but . . ." which is just another way of saying no.)

Try this in your next conversation:

- Begin each sentence with "Yes, and . . ." and then add an idea to the first idea. Don't get caught limiting yourself. Don't say "no" or "that's not possible." Go with it and see where it goes.

LISTEN WITH YOUR WHOLE BODY

How many times have we heard the phrase "You're listening, but you're not hearing what I am saying"? Active listening tunes your antennae to really focus on what is being communicated from others. Clear your mind and really try to understand what others are feeling and thinking. This builds empathy, which makes people feel validated.

Try this in your next conversation:

- Everyone is going to help tell a story using one word per person. Start with the words "Once upon a time." Then each person adds one word as you go around the room. Go around a few times, and then bring the story to an end.

HAVE EACH OTHER'S BACK

One of the great traditions of improvisation occurs before the ensemble walks onstage. Each player walks to everyone else in their cast, looks them in their eye, and says, "I've got your back." This simple exercise lets everyone know they will support each other no matter what happens or however crazy an idea is suggested.

Try this:

- How can you show support for your family or co-workers and make them feel empowered?

- What do others do to make you feel supported?

- How do you *feel* when you're supported?

YOUR FOCUS DETERMINES YOUR DIRECTION

Tony Robbins has a great saying: "Most of us major in minor things." We need to understand the value of what we're focusing on, whether it's an emotion or a task. Our focus is the most important tool we have.

You want to remember four incredibly important things about focus:

1. You'll always veer towards what you focus on. It's like riding a bike. If you're focused on how a project will fail, it most definitely will fail. Focus on how you can make something a success.

2. You can change your focus through motion. Get active on something to get your focus off something else. Nothing draws the mind into a laser beam of focus like getting physical.

4. Stop multitasking. It's not a thing. You're just switching between things quickly and serving them poorly. Try time-blocking instead. Work on one thing without interruptions for an hour.

Hey! What happened to #3? (Sorry, we were multitasking. Here it is!)

3. Manage your attitude through your focus. If you're feeling an emotion that isn't helping you get your work done, then change your focus. Do something silly for sixty seconds. Balance a pencil on your thumb. Touch your elbow to your nose. Quickly name your third-grade teachers — including the gym teacher.

Be present ... now ... and now ... and now.

Live in the Moment

Living "in" the moment is different than living "for" the moment. Many of us get lost in the regrets of the past or the fear of the future.

Newsflash: The past doesn't exert pressure over you and the future doesn't exist yet, so that just leaves the present.

Good improvisers live "in" the moment, which means they are 100 percent present in the moment they are currently experiencing. Being present in the moment means focusing on what's happening right now and looking to make it as wonderful as this moment can be.

Try this:

- When you let the past and the future start commenting on and impacting the present, we call that "being in your head" or not open to the abundance of your reality. Try doing a quick meditation exercise: picture yourself writing the thought invading your brain on a yellow sticky note and put it on the wall inside your head. Acknowledge that it is a thought and you will attend to it later. Now get back into the moment. And don't just be in the moment at work. Practice being present for your family and significant others.

You'll be amazed how much more you'll find to talk about or enjoy simple occasions when you're both present for the conversation.

FINAL THOUGHT

Walking out on that stage to improvise and play with Stephen Colbert and Amy Sedaris and eventually Steve Carell, Tina Fey, Matt Walsh, Amy Poehler, Rachel Dratch, Horatio Sans, Matt Walsh, and so many others was the most fun I've ever had as a performer. But only the beginning of how much fun improvisation would be in real life.

The Players Workshop, where I learned all of these magnificent life skills, closed in 2005. Before she passed away, I spoke with the school's founder, Josephine Forsberg, about how important these life lessons had become to me and how I had shared them with so many others. She said, "I've been waiting for someone to come along and reopen the Players Workshop. I believe you're that person."

Well, you guessed it. Eventually, I reopened the school to make sure everyone who wanted to learn these skills would be able to take classes at Players Workshop. Go to PlayersWorkshopOnline.com to check it out and take a virtual class.

A growth mindset is defined as the belief that the ability to learn is not fixed, because people with a growth mindset don't believe that failure is a permanent position. Neither do I. Instead, I believe in "win or learn," not "win or lose." I believe that a growth mindset is developed through learning and experience, which is exactly what improvisation gives you.

Adapt your mindset and be a playmaker!

Good luck and remember … I've got your back.

As an added bonus for buying this amazing book, I want to give you something else of value: would you be interested in a free course so you can instantly think faster?

Then you should take advantage of my course, *Instantly Think Faster*, which usually retails for $97, but I am giving it to you for free because you bought this book.

Download the ITF course and a few other free surprises at www.JeffRogersUnlimited.com.

Thank you, and remember to play!

About Jeff Rogers

If you've ever thought of the perfect thing to say ... twenty minutes after you wanted to say it, then you suffer from "slow-reaction-itis." Don't worry, there is a cure — become a playmaker!

Improvisation evangelist Jeff Rogers loves to teach people how to unleash their potential and move from being a Nervous Nellie to a passionate playmaker. He is the best-selling author of *The Playmaker Mindset*, the playbook for instant innovation, team building, and engagement. Jeff went from dropping out of college and working construction to performing onstage with Stephen Colbert, Steve Carell, Tina Fey, and Amy Sedaris at The Second City and eventually to co-creating, executive producing and hosting cable TV's award-winning *Homemade Game Show*.

Jeff is also the owner and managing partner of Players Workshop, the original school of improvisation in the United States. Players Workshop has taught over 10,000 students to be fearless "in the moment." He is a sought-after speaker on the topics of innovation, team building, and employee engagement.

CHAPTER 15:

ENTREPRENEURS CHANGING THE WORLD

BY KELLI NGUYEN-HA

I am the "grateful one." Because of my gratitude for the opportunity I was given in the U.S. I devoted myself to giving back and serving those who desire my specialized services in business and real estate finance, especially women.

I launched my new finance service, Lotus Commercial Capital Inc., during the coronavirus pandemic. I was able to help many women-owned businesses that were affected by it. My mission is to consult, support, and empower women-owned businesses, as well as real estate investors and developers with suitable options in flexible, creative, diversified, specialized, alternative financing solutions — both in equity and in debt financing options. Since 2008, I have also helped passive investors in private lending opportunities secured by real estate.

I believe entrepreneurs and small businesses are the lifeblood of the U.S. economy, and they historically have been underserved financially with limited available options (be it active, passive, equity, debts, or a combination of two or more of these) to choose what's the best fit for their financial goals. I've been in the trenches and experienced the entrepreneur world most of my life. I actually grew up in a family of small businesses.

My parents came to the U.S. with a little bit of gold, and without a single word of English, on December 18, 1978. My dad started out as a full-time welder. Part-time, he learned another trade in the shrimping business until he was ready to acquire one small shrimp boat, and eventually acquired larger boats. When he had captains running all seven of his boats, he stayed on land to start other businesses. My father went from land to sea to land and started a small restaurant. Once that was successful, he sold it and started an Asian grocery store. This went from being a small location to being the largest Asian foods market in Port Arthur, Texas.

At the age of ten, I started helping my parents. I learned the struggle. I fully understand it from my experience as the daughter of immigrant parents and living through their experience in a new country. And from them, I learned important lessons. For the purposes of this chapter, I want to share with you the importance of asset protection/insurance, the effects of operating with a lack of access to capital or resources, and how to maximize tax benefits.

LESSON 1: ASSET PROTECTION/INSURANCE

My dad spoke zero words of English when he arrived in the U.S. He needed to learn enough to support his wife and eight children. Because his language was limited, he depended on translators for all his business dealings, which meant trusting anyone who helped him in his transactions.

He paid cash for insurance, in which there were policies for all seven boats, and his payments went directly to the agent. Thinking everything was taken care of, my father leaned on trust and continued operating for five years. Long story short, the agent took my dad's money for himself and never purchased insurance for my dad.

While there were no claims or issues in those first five years, in 1986, there came a day when one of his boats sank during a storm. His captain and the entire crew were thankfully saved by the Coast Guard, but the largest shrimp boat was lost to the ocean. He should have been compensated for this, according to the policies discussed. However, it was at that point that my dad discovered the insurance agent had robbed his hard-blood-sweat-and-tears-earned money.

In 1987, one year after the storm, my mother was diagnosed with stage IV cervical cancer. She had only five years at most to live. My dad's focus shifted from businesses to getting my mom better. One by one, he needed to sell all of his businesses. At the time, they didn't have health insurance. All of my parents' businesses were sold to sustain my mom's life through the vigorous and daunting diagnostic procedures, hospitalizations, and treatments (chemotherapies, radiation, and so on).

LESSON 2: LACK OF ACCESS TO CAPITAL AND RESOURCES

My parents started all their businesses with their own saved, hard-earned money. Many business owners are similar to my parents, in that they lack the understanding of their credit status and borrowing options. In business and financing, it's all about knowing your options based on your unique situation, like your credit, collateral, industry, geographic region, company revenues, profits, and so on. All these things impact what you can and can't do.

Once you understand business and financing, there are many different ways to get money for your business or projects. But they all fall into one of two basic categories: you're either (1) giving up equity in your business or (2) taking on debt. In the space of financing, you must decide whether you want your funding through debt or equity — or, in some cases, a combination of the two.

Most real estate investors and developers and business owners need financing to start, build, and grow their businesses. When acquired and used properly, financing is a great leverage vehicle to achieve your goals and dreams. Acquiring financing incorrectly or using it poorly, however, will hinder your business's cash flow, damage your business relationships, and hurt your chances of business success and growing your portfolio.

For real estate investors and business owners, cash flow is king. When seeking capital, you want to ensure that it is cash flow friendly. By working with a trusted advisor who understands the ins and outs of business and financing (equity or debts structures), you greatly increase your chances of not only getting the financing you need today, but also positioning your business/project to obtain the financing you may need to scale and expand in the future. A clear understanding of your borrowing options allows you to make the best decision and get the lowest-cost form of capital based on your options. Then it's about taking action on the one or more options now available to you.

Theodore Roosevelt once said, "In any moment of decision, the best thing you can do is the right thing, the next best thing is the wrong thing, and the worst thing you can do is nothing." I love this quote because my father taught me that it is not what we learn that makes a difference in our lives, but what we do with what we learned.

LESSON 3: MAXIMIZE YOUR TAX BENEFITS

My parents weren't aware of this strategy at all. The vast majority of people miss out on tax benefits because they don't borrow or leverage money the right way. Different investment vehicles come with different tax shelters. That's why you need to understand how and when to leverage to maximize your tax benefits.

Do you think the wealthy write off all the money they borrow for their businesses and all the money they received from their investments?

Why don't you?

Of course, you need to consult with the right CPA and the right legal and tax professionals for the details. I advise you to do so as soon as possible.

FEEDBACK FROM PAST CLIENTS

One of the individuals with the highest integrity from my business journey is Mr. Otokar Benke. He's an immigrant from Slovakia and a retired executive from Toshiba. We were initially introduced by a family friend of sixteen years, former business partner Michael Chung. After working together, Benke had this to say:

> "I tested Kelli out in 2009, by just giving her my very first investment was a $68,502.78 private loan secured by real estate. I don't just trust anyone and I am very cautious with my hard-earned money. Kelli did all the work and I earned a monthly income of 10% interest on my money, paid to me each and every month, never missing a beat to this day.
>
> Kelli and I became friends and she treated me like her own family. She always expressed her gratitude toward me, but instead I am the one who feels grateful for her hard work. Kelli has a network of passive investors at her fingertips, but she chooses to only build relationships with a handful of those she likes and trusts.
>
> Over 10 years, Kelli has shown me nothing less than a highly respected and trusted individual who has her investor as her priority. No matter what happens, she makes sure that I get my money first. If there was a loss due to unforeseen circumstances, she absorbed those losses herself.
>
> Not only is Kelli's capability as a real estate investor/ developer and her business expertise impressive, more importantly, she's very compassionate and has the utmost respect and integrity. She cares not only about just her win, but the win for her investors, who remain her priority.
>
> To me, working with Kelli over the years has proven to me that I've made the smartest choice of growing my money with no work involved. And it sure pays me very

well. In fact, it pays ten times — yes, ten multiples — more than what I've earned from the bank prior to her.

Since then, I've brought Kelli my sister and my close friends who had similar investment goals as mine. We enjoyed our average 10% interest on all our investments secured by real estate. Combined together, we have invested over $3 million with Kelli over the last ten years. We invested in a total of twenty-five projects and most of them have returned our capital. We re-invested as it matured.

I am grateful to Kelli for my peace of mind. I retired from Toshiba in 2018 and have been able to travel back to my country at will for months at a time without needing to worry about the related cost like most of my colleagues. And I'm not only grateful for my wife and I, but my sister in Slovakia living off of her interest earned payments by this passive investment. I've also been able to support my extended family financially for the last five years as well. I wouldn't be in this situation today without Kelli's true compassion and kindness toward her investors."

Two sisters, Sally and Mary Trahan, once owned a full-service salon and spa in Houston, Texas. They worked really hard to establish a total of three salons from their own hard-earned money. They are very good at the service they provide for their clients.

After working with me, Sally said the following:

"We owe so much to Kelli. She spent countless hours with us to help us figure out the best solutions that fit best for our business situation. It's good to be aware of so many options, but at the same time, without Kelli's compassion, patience, and devotion to us to having a most suited outcome, we wouldn't have known what to do or which is best for us. She thoroughly explained all our options and reasons. Not only did she help us obtain the lowest fee/interest options for our immediate capital need, she was also working with us to prepare our business to be in a constant state of readiness for capital, scale, and future growth.

Most importantly, we are now financially prepared and ready to endure any crisis. Before we met Kelli, we only used our own saved money and that quickly ran out when we were forced to shut down all our businesses in March this year (2020). However, with Kelli, we continue to have the same overhead despite the no revenue during closure."

And Mary said:

"I've not met a person that's more knowledgeable in business and in finance options than Kelli. She is well-rounded, from how to calculate the numbers to acquire all the way to the right funding options best for cash flow focus, individual focus, or net profit focus on exiting the stabilized project. But yet Kelli is very humble, kind-hearted, and truly cares for the best outcome for our business success and survival, short-term and long-term. I feel grateful to have found Kelli, especially during this health pandemic.

We were recommended to Kelli through a few of our friends. Kristine Meyer was helped by Kelli in acquiring a self-storage facility through an SBA 7a loan. Kelli also helped our friend, Julie Truong, with a bridge loan to acquire a value-add shopping center and refinance into a non-recourse CMBS loan once stabilized. And for another friend, Mariann Jones, Kelli helped her acquire 140 key Economy Lodge hotels with private money and refinance into a conventional loan upon stabilization."

CLEAR AND FOCUSED

In closing, I share another favorite quote of mine, by Benjamin Franklin: "By failing to prepare, you are preparing to fail."

I maintain an attitude of allowing nothing to get in the way of my clear, focused plan of actions to obtain my long-term and short-term goals. I don't have time for non-relevant excuses such as being an immigrant, a female, physically challenged at only 4'11", or speaking English as a second language, or even business and real estate investing/development belonging only to men. Et cetera, et cetera.

Yes, female entrepreneurs, real estate investors/developers, and business owners have less access to capital than men. Does that stop me? No.

Yes, women were 32 percent more likely than men to receive a subprime mortgage, regardless of income[5] — despite women having better credit scores and disparity. Will that stop you?

The year 2020 has been one of the most challenging years in history for small businesses and real estate investors/developers across America. Meanwhile, I've established an extended family through building a business relationship with individuals. As I've shared here, I'm mostly focused on helping women-owned businesses and female real estate investors/developers in my journey.

Whether it's my passive investor clients, clients I've helped obtain PPP, EIDL, and SBA working capital loans, or clients I help obtain creative/alternative financing, I've not only helped them to sustain their business during the coronavirus pandemic, but to prepare their business for growth.

The most important financial story of the next decade will be how entrepreneurs — especially women — consolidate our century of economic gains. It will be how they focus our financial clout, placing our own "ownership" stamp on how businesses, services, and values are driven to create a better world for all.

5. Ping Cheng, Zhenguo Lin & Yingchun Liu, "Do Women Pay More for Mortgages?", *The Journal of Real Estate Finance and Economics* vol. 43 (2011): 423–440, https://link.springer.com/article/10.1007/s11146-009-9214-y.

About Kelli Nguyen-Ha

In 2002, Kelli Nguyen-Ha retired from her last position in the health care industry as a DON (director of nursing), overseeing three units (ICU, CCU, and telemetry), in pursuit of her dream of being an entrepreneur.

Kelli is now an entrepreneur, a residential and commercial real estate investor, hotel developer, and business transformation expert. She has experience in both hotel and short-term rental developments in Texas, Arizona, and Georgia, as well as self-storage and retail shopping center redevelopment in Tennessee, Florida, and Ohio.

She is a wife, a mother, a sister to her seven siblings, and a niece to the only uncle she grew up with in the U.S., serving in place of her deceased parents.

Kelli is also the author of the book *Immigrant Millionaire: The Story of One Asian Woman Obsessed to Succeed in the Land of Opportunity*. She can be reached through the websites www.LuxLodgingpro.com and www.LotusComCap.com.

CHAPTER 16:

THE QUIET EPIDEMIC

BY DR. RICHARD KELLEY, MD

"I'm scared. I keep having pains in my chest," she said.

We ran all the tests available to us in the hospital emergency room, test after test, but nothing seemed to be wrong with her heart.

What could be the source of her pain?

The CT scan of her chest looked normal, but the radiologist pointed out "fatty infiltration of the liver."

Fatty liver. I knew what *that* meant.

I asked her, "Did your doctor tell you that your liver enzymes are elevated?"

"No, he said I was healthy."

Our tests showed nothing wrong with her heart, so she was released from the hospital without treatment. But she was in her mid-thirties and weighed over 275 pounds — a far cry from what I would consider "healthy."

A healthy weight for her height probably would have been around 135 pounds, so her body was under the stress of managing double her weight — the equivalent of carrying around an extra person.

Her experience is not isolated. For almost a decade, I ran a weight loss clinic and I would see patients every day who would complain of "strange" symptoms:

- vague feelings of pain or discomfort;
- trouble getting out of bed in the morning;
- dozing off during the day;
- unexplained rashes or patches of dark skin;
- feeling irritable for no apparent reason;
- finding themselves easily distracted.

WHY IS THIS A PROBLEM?

People who are anywhere from 50 to 150 pounds overweight often can't tell where their pain is coming from. They don't realize that, over time, being overweight and being obese are quietly killing them.

They also don't realize there's *one thing* that could help them restore their health and diminish the likelihood of similar emergency room visits in the future.

As an ER physician with twenty years of experience, I've developed a keen sense of intuition, but I still rely on data for proof. I run tests and search for answers backed by science.

Frequently, almost everything shows "within normal limits" for my overweight or obese patients. So without explanation, they are released from the hospital.

But something still isn't quite right. And that's why I asked my ER patient about her elevated liver enzymes.

Having run a weight loss clinic for almost a decade, I knew that elevated liver enzymes and fatty liver were signs that my patient with chest pain was well on her way to becoming a type 2 diabetic.

Type 2 diabetes is insidious. Left unchecked, it can cause blindness, kidney damage, hearing impairment, and even disability due to amputations of the feet and lower extremities.

It is a precursor to Alzheimer's and dementia, which are progressive and irreversible. These diseases destroy memory and thinking skills. In advanced stages, they make independent living impossible.

And it's now the leading cause of heart disease, which kills more Americans than any other cause of death.

Pre- and type 2 diabetes often go undetected for years, eventually wreaking havoc on every single system in the body. No organ system goes untouched.

This is terrible news for the tens of millions of Americans who will develop type 2 diabetes this year.

BUT THERE IS GOOD NEWS

Type 2 diabetes can be reversed, and there's one thing that has a success rate of nearly 100 percent.

I'll share that secret soon, but first, let me share with you what I learned as a very green surgical intern at a large trauma hospital in Louisiana back in 1993. I'll never forget the question the chief resident asked me.

"What does MD stand for?"

"It stands for 'medical doctor,'" I said.

"No. That's not what it means … at least not *here*. MD, in the world you're in now — in this surgery program — stands for '*make decisions.*'

"You're going to be faced with emergent patient situations every single day, and you're going to have to address them. If you can't make decisions and act in *this* environment, you're not going to survive in the world of medicine, and your patients will suffer in the process."

Those words never left me.

Even now, I have a decision to make. The Latin root of "decision" is "cis." It's also in "scissors," and it means "to cut." I must decide which content to cut and which specific topics to cover.

My medical experience spans three decades, from general surgery to emergency medicine, from family practice to obesity medicine. I could have chosen almost any topic, but I knew I needed to sound the alarm on what I call "the quiet epidemic" — type 2 diabetes, a disease primarily brought on by excess weight.

Growing up through the 1960s and '70s and entering medical school in the late '80s, I've observed a drastic transformation in our country over the past six decades.

Our patient population is getting heavier and heavier.

I was a high school student in the '70s. Back then, few of us were overweight, a reality that mirrored the population at large. But that's all changed within the past fifty years.

I could sit back and watch the problem continue to grow, or I could do something about it.

I made the decision with my wife Sherrill to open a fitness and weight-management clinic in Austin, Texas, helping thousands of men and women lose weight and regain their health.

During the years we operated that clinic, I noticed something unusual — something I was uniquely qualified to address.

Almost every weight-management patient had elevated liver enzymes (ALT and AST). Though I'd see the same elevated enzymes in the ER in overweight and obese patients, there I had the benefit of obtaining additional studies.

CT and ultrasound frequently showed these patients to have fatty infiltration of the liver, as well as diabetic skin changes — despite having normal blood glucose levels.

The same patients had often been told by their doctors that they were healthy because their blood glucose was normal — even if they were 50 to 100 or more pounds overweight!

But what I came to understand is that these fatty liver changes represented the origins of insulin resistance, and that meant they were poised to develop type 2 diabetes.

Because it's a progressive process, and being overweight or obese has become normal, people don't realize the underlying damage that's being done over time.

According to recent statistics from the Centers for Disease Control and Prevention (CDC), over 34 million Americans (just over one in ten) have diabetes, and 90–95 percent of those cases are type 2 diabetes.[6]

Even more alarming is that almost 20 percent of children ages 2–19 are not just overweight, but reportedly obese.[7]

---

6. "Type 2 Diabetes," Centers for Disease Control and Prevention, last reviewed: May 30, 2019, https://www.cdc.gov/diabetes/basics/type2.html.

7. "Childhood Obesity Facts," Centers for Disease Control and Prevention, last reviewed: June 24, 2019, https://www.cdc.gov/obesity/data/childhood.html.

Truly, This Is an Epidemic of Staggering Proportions

In a nutshell, type 2 diabetes keeps the patients' blood glucose and insulin level chronically elevated, and they end up with damage to blood vessels that feed the heart, the eyes, the kidneys, and the nerves.

Even the stomach and gastrointestinal tract can be affected because impairment of the nerves to the stomach can prevent food from moving throughout the GI tract efficiently.

It's common for chronic diabetic foot ulcers to develop and get infected because they heal slowly, if at all. That can lead to amputation of the feet or lower legs.

The whole body is at risk of major damage if something doesn't change.

What I discovered is that if *one thing* changed — if the patient could just commit to losing their excess weight — then the symptoms of type 2 diabetes would eventually disappear.

The truth is that roughly 90 percent of all diabetes in the United States is linked to excess weight.[8] But this parameter is overwhelmingly minimized from a treatment standpoint at the hands of traditional medicine.

Dr. Jason Fung, author of *The Diabetes Code: Prevent and Reverse Type 2 Diabetes Naturally*, says that because we as doctors were largely ineffective in helping patients lose weight, we eventually threw up our hands and began referring to type 2 diabetes as a chronic, incurable disease and began treating this diet and lifestyle-based disorder with ever-increasing doses of prescription medications.

What's the Big Deal?

It's now more common for Americans to be overweight — or even obese — than it is to be at an ideal weight. CDC statistics from 2016 show only 30 percent of American adults at a normal weight, which means that over 70 percent of the American adult population was overweight. That number continues to climb.

---

8. Alvin Powell, "Obesity? Diabetes? We've been set up," *The Harvard Gazette*, March 7, 2012, https://news.harvard.edu/gazette/story/2012/03/the-big-setup/.

It may seem normal to be overweight, but it's not. Being overweight leads to pre- and type 2 diabetes, the quiet epidemic.

While 88 million American adults (more than one in three) have prediabetes, almost 74 million of these people don't even know they have it![9]

This is an enormous problem, but it doesn't even speak to or address the number of children and young adults who are overweight, obese, and pre- or type 2 diabetic at younger ages, and in greater number, than have *ever* been recorded in history.

And the problem isn't exclusive to America. Obesity and type 2 diabetes represent a growing, global epidemic.

WHO CAN HELP SOLVE THIS PROBLEM?

You might think that the medical field would have all the tools necessary to address this growing epidemic, but as physicians treating type 2 diabetics with medication, we are mostly making people fatter, not better!

The sad fact is that most medications used to treat type 2 diabetics, with the overarching goal of decreasing blood glucose and A1C, actually accelerate weight gain and worsen the disease in the process.

It's clear to me that the solution to being overweight, being obese, and having type 2 diabetes will ultimately come from visionaries and entrepreneurs — as well as doctors who are coloring outside the lines of what they were taught in medical school.

Family physician Dr. Ken Berry, author of *Lies My Doctor Told Me,* is one of a handful of voices out of thousands of physicians in the United States who preaches the merits and benefits of low carb and ketogenic nutrition. He leads his patients and followers by example.

Orthopedic surgeon Dr. Shawn Baker challenges conventional dietary dogma with his book *The Carnivore Diet.* Though controversial to many, those who follow his meat-focused dietary approach are losing weight and getting fit while most Americans are gaining weight and getting sick on the Standard American Diet (SAD).

9. "Prediabetes – Your Chance to Prevent Type 2 Diabetes," Centers for Disease Control and Prevention, last reviewed: June 11, 2020, https://www.cdc.gov/diabetes/basics/prediabetes.html.

Each of these doctors has chosen to evaluate what they were taught during medical training. They've acknowledged that the traditional medical approach to obesity, type 2 diabetes, and other lifestyle disorders is broken. And they're offering their take on approaches to reverse them.

And guess what? Despite criticism, they're all having success in areas where traditional medical treatments have failed.

On a broader scale, the ultimate answer to our obesity and type 2 diabetes problems may come from those who have made living in a healthy body a way of life.

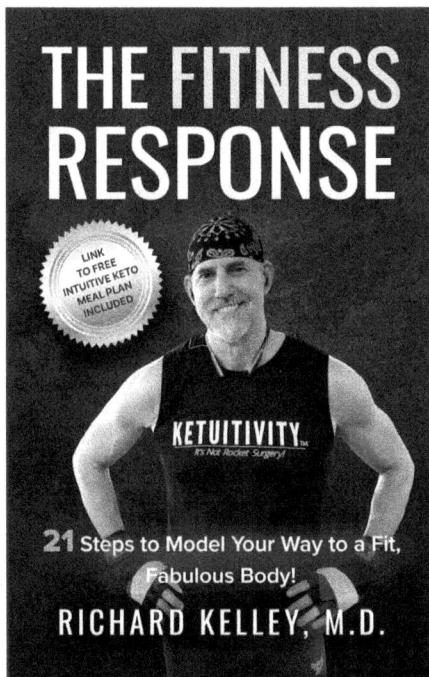

In my book *The Fitness Response*, I encourage readers to follow entrepreneurs, coaches, personal trainers, and those who model a lifestyle of health and fitness. These are the leaders who are poised to play a pivotal role in altering the tide of the greatest silent plague of the 21st century.

The focus of my own program, Type 2 To Health®, is to offer those dealing with pre- and type 2 diabetes a path not only to weight loss but also to physical transformation.

Time and again, I've seen patients who make their health a priority reverse the diabetic markers of disease.

Good health can be modeled. The body can be physically transformed. This reality is possible through the dedicated, consistent implementation of a strategic fitness and nutrition plan.

Most contemporary practicing doctors who "grew up in medicine" went through their training after 1980. They experienced the full impact of a failed national push for low-fat, low-calorie diets and the absurdly flawed food pyramid of the 1990s, as well as the indoctrination of pharmaceutical propaganda and medical dogma which still conveys the erroneous message that type 2 diabetes is a chronic, nonreversible disease.

Big Pharma has completely hijacked the narrative surrounding the treatment of type 2 diabetes to the point that blood glucose and hemoglobin A1C have become the primary targets to be managed.

Big Pharma, the manufactured food industry, and prescribing doctors, which are promoted by our nation's media, all contribute to this quiet epidemic rather than fight it.

If you need to lose weight to get healthier, but your doctor is adamant that type 2 diabetes can't be reversed, it's important to understand that your doctor is a guide, not a god.

If you're gaining weight despite medical treatment for type 2 diabetes, it's time to try a different approach. Find a physician who has had success with a more holistic approach to this disorder.

YOU ARE NOT HELPLESS

There is a way forward for you and your loved ones to become healthier. And guess what? *You* get to make the decision. Do you want to model those who have achieved wellness and vitality? Do you want to live a long, healthy, active life?

Then commit to a daily plan of fitness. Optimize your nutrition. Don't simply rely on traditional medical approaches which have been such a dismal failure (and are actually making type 2 diabetes worse).

Read the books by the doctors I've mentioned. Though their approaches may fly in the face of what you've been taught, their patients, clients, and followers are seeing results in areas where traditional medicine has failed.

SEEK OUT MODELS OF SUCCESS

Find those who have the health, fitness, and body you'd ideally like to have, and find out what they did to achieve the results you desire. Seek out entrepreneurs whose mission it is to help others become fit and healthy again.

My hope is for you to live in the healthiest body possible. My desire is to encourage and empower doctors and entrepreneurs who are taking nontraditional approaches to reverse so-called nonreversible disorders.

Let's turn the tide on this silent and insidious epidemic.

You are the primary maker of your personal health.

May the years to come be your healthiest and most vibrant.

ABOUT DR. RICHARD KELLEY, MD

Dr. Kelley is an emergency physician based in Austin, Texas, whose passions include fitness and entrepreneurship.

He is the author of *The Fitness Response: 21 Steps to Model Your Way to a Fit, Fabulous Body*, as well as his most recent book, *Wealth, Fitness, & Power for Life*.

As a physician, Dr. Kelley encourages others to make exercise and optimal nutrition daily non-negotiables. He is the founder of Type 2 To Health˚, a program designed to help his clients reverse pre- and type 2 diabetes through weight loss, lifestyle changes, and the ongoing pursuit of physical transformation.

Throughout his career, Dr. Kelley has helped thousands of men and women lose weight and achieve a greater level of health. He strives to be a model of the lifestyle he promotes.

For more information about the programs and resources that Dr. Kelley has to offer, visit www.RichardKelleyMD.com or Type2ToHealth.com.

CHAPTER 17:

YOUR REAL WEALTH IS YOUR HEALTH
(THE ENTREPRENEUR'S ACCELERATED GUIDELINES FOR OPTIMAL HEALTH, ENERGY, AND VITALITY)

BY DR. ATOUSA MAHDAVI,
HOLISTIC DOCTOR, SPEAKER, AND AUTHOR

Growing up, I was always drawn to older relatives who were sick or suffering from ailments, especially after the death of my maternal grandfather when I was only four, whom I was really close to. When I was five or six, observing my paternal grandmother suffering from rheumatoid arthritis, I would offer to rub her pain ointment on her wrists. As similar situations kept presenting themselves throughout my life, a deep sense of curiosity with a strong passion for understanding the human mechanics of health grew stronger and stronger. A great sense of desire grew within me to help relieve the suffering of others.

Our world changed fast, especially for entrepreneurs, during the 2020-2021 pandemic. With the disruption of commerce and massive economical setbacks for entrepreneurs and small business owners, as well as disruptions of social connections, our lives have been altered in profound ways. This global pandemic makes one thing abundantly clear: your health needs to be a priority. We no longer have the luxury of postponing it. It's not just someday, but right now.

During this viral pandemic, our mortality has become apparent to us like never before. But we also hear the statistics about how the majority of those losing their lives are suffering from chronic health conditions and comorbidities. It is not a surprise that our underlying health issues have a profound impact on our body's ability to respond to illnesses of all kinds — including COVID-19.

The data is in, and the science is clear. People with underlying conditions like heart disease, obesity, asthma, autoimmune disease, and type 2 diabetes are more vulnerable to viruses like COVID-19. According to the CDC, in July 2020, only 6 percent of deaths were caused by COVID-19 alone; for the remaining percentage, on average, there were 2.6 additional conditions or causes per death in addition to COVID-19. That means that, on average, 94 percent of people who died from COVID-19 had 2.6 additional health conditions at the time of their death.

The truth is that we are going through a health pandemic in this country. Let's look at the numbers:

- We have, as of 2018, 34.2 million people diagnosed with diabetes (that is, 10.5 percent of the U.S. population).[10]

- According to the CDC, from 1999–2000 through 2017–2018, the prevalence of obesity increased from 30.5 percent to 42.4 percent.[11]

- According to the National Institute of Mental Health (NIH) in 2017, an estimated 2.3 million adolescents aged 12 to 17 in the United States had at least one major depressive episode with severe impairment. This number represented 9.4 percent of the U.S. population aged 12 to 17.[12]

---

10. "Statistics About Diabetes," American Diabetes Association, last accessed January 24, 2021, https://www.diabetes.org/resources/statistics/statistics-about-diabetes.

11. "Adult Obesity Facts," Centers for Disease Control and Prevention, last reviewed June 29, 2020, https://www.cdc.gov/obesity/data/adult.html.

12. "Major Depression," National Institute of Mental Health, last updated February 2019, https://www.nimh.nih.gov/health/statistics/major-depression.shtml.

- According to the CDC, one person dies every 36 seconds in the United States from cardiovascular disease. About 655,000 Americans die from heart disease each year — that's one in every four deaths.[13]

- According to the *American Journal of Medicine* in 2020, cancer is the second leading cause of death in the United States, with researchers from the American Cancer Society predicting the disease will affect more than 1.7 million people and cause 600,000 deaths in the nation this year.[14]

- According to the CDC, in 2019, more than 67,000 people died from drug overdoses in 2018, making it a leading cause of injury-related death in the United States. Of those deaths, almost 70 percent involved a prescription or illicit opioid.[15]

The modern diet, the toxic food culture, and the unhealthy lifestyle and mindset, in addition to stress and environmental toxicities, are the driving forces behind epidemic rates of heart disease, cancer, type 2 diabetes, obesity, asthma, and hypertension.

The good news is that all these conditions are preventable by simply having a healthy lifestyle and diet, as well as a right mindset. When you give the body the right nutrients and a healthy environment internally and externally, then the body can heal itself.

Professionals and entrepreneurs are sometimes more prone to self-neglect and lack of self-care as they get wrapped up in the daily grind of their work and business, many times under an enormous amount of stress.

---

13. "Heart Disease Facts," Centers for Disease Control and Prevention, last reviewed September 8, 2020, https://www.cdc.gov/heartdisease/facts.htm.

14. Matthew Gavidia, "Overall US Cancer Mortality Rate Reaches 26-Year Decline, but Obesity-Relaed Cancer Deaths Rise," *American Journal of Medicine* (January 8, 2020), https://www.ajmc.com/view/overall-us-cancer-mortality-rate-reaches-26year-decline-but-obesityrelated-cancer-deaths-rise.

15. Holly Hedegaard, MD, Arialdi M. Miniño, MPH, and Margaret Warner, PhD, "Drug Overdose Deaths in the United States, 1999–2018," NCHS Data Brief no. 356 (January 2020), Centers for Disease Control and Prevention, last reviewed January 30, 2020, https://www.cdc.gov/nchs/products/databriefs/db356.htm.

A good example was my patient Oliver, a 35-year-old corporate professional, who was forty pounds overweight and prediabetic, lacked energy, and was experiencing anxiety. By following simple actionable steps such as eating the right foods for his constitution and having the right nutrition and daily routines with proper self-care, he lost 30 pounds in three months, his A1C went back to normal, and he now has more energy and his anxiety has resolved.

When your health is optimal, you are more productive. This will naturally boost productivity and morale, both for the self-employed entrepreneur and the corporate professional. This in turn results in mental and emotional stability, which is the prerequisite to managing stress and the motivation to create a healthy lifestyle resulting in optimal health. With an optimized state of physical, emotional, and mental health, your immune system will be enhanced, as the body functions as an interconnected system. The lifestyle principles and guidelines that I offer you in this chapter are geared towards optimizing your health, energy, and immune system, with specific attention to managing cold and flu symptoms.

THE ENTREPRENEUR'S DAILY ROUTINES AND SELF-CARE, BASED ON CIRCADIAN RHYTHM AND AYURVEDA

During this pandemic, many are working from home and children are homeschooled. This has resulted in a lack of a set schedule which disturbs the regular daily routines, in turn disrupting the physiological biorhythms set forth by nature. Lacking a set daily routine is a recipe for a lack of energy, stress, digestive issues, anxiety, and insomnia, all of which can weaken the immune system. Some of the perils of this pandemic are mental health issues and challenges stemming from stress, energy deficiency, and anxiety, which is also associated with a lack of daily routine, self-care, and healthy rituals.

These recommended daily routines and self-care rituals are based on circadian rhythms and Ayurvedic medicine, aligned with the physiological time stamps, making it possible to live in harmony with nature.

- Wake up between six to seven a.m.; melatonin goes down, cortisol begins to rise, sharpest rise in blood pressure.

- After brushing and flossing your teeth, inspect your tongue for a yellow, green, white, or brown coating which is digestive toxins (Ama). Scrape it off before it can be reabsorbed, using a tongue scraper, preferably one made out of stainless steel or copper.

- Oil pulling: Swish one tablespoon of sesame or coconut oil around in your mouth for sixty seconds (avoid swallowing). When done, spit the oil into a paper towel and place in the trash to avoid having the oil clogging your pipes.

- As soon as you start having a scratchy or sore throat, start gargling with salt water and turmeric three to four times a day.

- Drink one or two cups of room-temperature water with a squeeze of lemon upon waking up. If you have constipation, flu, or cold symptoms, then warm water is preferred.

Set the Tone and Intention for the Day

- Make time for a minimum of ten to twenty minutes of breathing meditation, exercise, or yoga, all of which trigger the release of the feel-good hormones, helping you cope with stress. If you don't have time, sit for five minutes of meditation, deep breathing, and focusing on three things you want to accomplish and three things you have gratitude for.

- The best time for bowel movements is seven to eight thirty a.m. or after the first meal. You must have at least one bowel movement a day.

- The best time for breakfast is between seven to eight a.m. Insulin secretion with the first meal is optimal at this time, but if you have no appetite, follow the intermittent fasting schedule below or have a small shake or smoothie (warm tea with honey if you have constipation, cold, or flu symptoms).

- Intermittent fasting is consuming two meals a day — the first meal between ten to eleven a.m. and the second meal at six p.m. If you feel hungry at midday, have a healthy snack like a piece of fruit with nut butter.

- The most productive time of the day is between ten a.m. and two p.m., when Pitta is high, with high alertness — the best time for productivity and business negotiations. The best time for lunch (if not intermittent fasting) according to Ayurveda is at noon, when Pitta is high, meaning there is a strong fire of digestion within the system, as the sun is at its peak at noon.

- The highest musculoskeletal strength is at five p.m.; allocate time for exercise or yoga, at least half an hour a day. An ideal exercise for half an hour would be an interval training exercise such as walking for ten minutes, followed by a short burst of running for two to five minutes, then repeat.

- The best time for dinner is between five to seven p.m. You need at least three hours between your last meal and bedtime.

- Go to sleep by ten p.m. Melatonin starts to rise at nine p.m. — this is the Kapha time in Ayurveda, which is dull and lazy. Do not watch TV, be on your phone, check your emails, or read in bed. Every hour before midnight equals two hours of sleep as opposed to after midnight.

- If you have a flu with mild fever (less than 100°F), take a warm bath with baking soda and or apple cider vinegar. With body aches, add Epsom salt to the bath water.

THE ENTREPRENEUR'S GENERAL GUIDELINES FOR HEALTHY FOOD CHOICES

Food is medicine, not only according to Ayurveda; there are many references in the Bible as well. Plan ahead for success by preparing your meals to avoid eating out.

40 to 60 percent of your meals should be vegetables and carbohydrates:

- Vegetables: choose mostly above-ground, green, leafy vegetables, and (in moderation) high-glycemic underground and tuber vegetables like potatoes and yams;

- Organic whole grains, oats, barley, basmati rice, millet, bulgur, amaranth, stone ground wheat, durum pasta;

- Low-glycemic whole fruits such as blueberries, apples, lemons and limes, plums, and pears, and less of high-glycemic whole fruits such as grapes, pineapple, and melons.

25 to 35 percent of your meals should be proteins:

- Nuts and seeds, nut butter such as almond butter (avoid peanut butter);

- Legumes such as lentils, mung beans, beans;

- Sprouts and quinoa;

- Cold-water fish, like salmon;

- Eggs: cage-free, pasture-raised, organic.

15 to 25 percent of your meals should contain fats:

- Nuts (almonds and walnuts) and seeds (pumpkin seed, sunflower seed), nut butter (almond butter and tahini), avocado, and coconut, coconut butter, organic butter, fish which also contains oils;

- Oils for cooking such as ghee, coconut oil, avocado oil;

- Extra-virgin olive oil, cold-pressed for salads or spread on food, but not for cooking.

THE ENTREPRENEUR'S GENERAL GUIDELINES FOR HEALTHY EATING

- Eat until you are 75 percent full.

- Eat fresh and organic food.

- Don't eat canned, processed, or packaged foods or TV dinners.

- Avoid microwave cooking.

- Avoid sodas and the junk food and snacks at the office.

- Avoid the snacks from the vending machines — take fruits and veggie sticks for snacks instead.

- Read the labels — avoid additives, preservatives, and artificial food coloring.

- Avoid excessive coffee drinking and juices with high sugar content.

WHEN YOU HAVE THE FLU

Eat more of these:

- Garlic (raw is best, with food);
- Green tea, ginger lemon tea with honey;
- Turmeric;
- Red onions;
- Thyme tea;
- Vegetables.

Avoid cold, heavy, and dry foods. Eat cooked, warm foods like soups and stews. Avoid drinking cold drinks. Also use and increase the amount of thermogenic spices in your cooking. Be sure to use cumin, black pepper, turmeric, fresh ginger, coriander, and cloves.

If you have a dry cough, do not skip your meals. If you do not have an appetite, have a vegetable broth with turmeric, salt, and fresh ginger and vegetables like leeks, kale, and bok choy or, alternatively, a soupy mixture of basmati white rice, salt, turmeric, and fresh ginger.

Supplements

It is recommended to take certain supplements to enhance the immune system and also as a preventative measure during the flu season. Some of these are zinc, vitamin C, quercetin, vitamin D3, echinacea, selenium, and melatonin.

Other supplements when experiencing cold or flu symptoms are goldenseal, holy basil, elderberry extract, cod liver oil, sage, and oil of oregano.

Herbal Steam Treatment for Cold and Flu

Herbal steam inhalation using a few drops of essential oils such as tea tree oil, sage, and eucalyptus oil is a very effective way of clearing and soothing the nasal and airway passages.

THE ENTREPRENEUR'S MINDSET PRACTICE

Without the proper mindset, our productivity is reduced, our energy is drained, and we cannot cope with stress. Stress is often referred to as a state of fight or flight. Essentially it is a mindset that is incapable of meeting the demands of work and life. The following practice will help you address this issue.

Breath Awareness to Reduce Anxiety, Tension, and Stress

Throughout the day, when a negative thought or emotion such as fear, anger, or helplessness arises and you are ready to either fight or flee, pause and take a deep, slow, and steady breath. Do not react as you normally would. Bring your attention to your breath. Pay attention to the sound of your breath, and also feel your abdomen rising and falling with each breath. Then replace the negative thought with a positive affirmation while you focus on your breath. Make a habit of watching your thoughts and the emotions triggered by them.

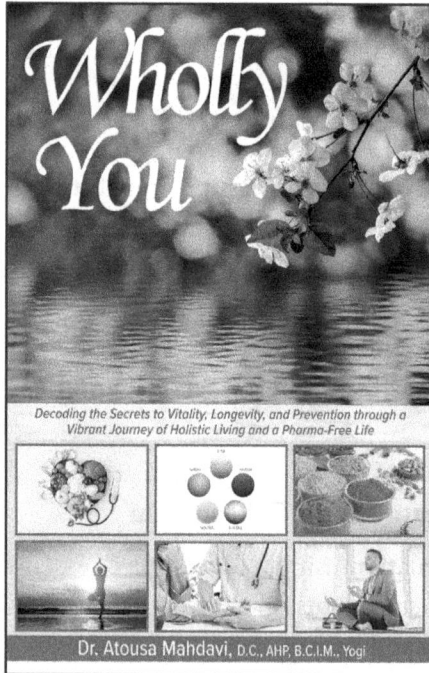

Wholly You

Decoding the Secrets to Vitality, Longevity, and Prevention through a Vibrant Journey of Holistic Living and a Pharma-Free Life

Dr. Atousa Mahdavi, D.C., AHP, B.C.I.M., Yogi

Conclusion

During the pandemic, many of my patients and I have been able to maintain our health and well-being by following these simple guidelines while keeping our businesses running. I have even managed to complete my book, *Wholly You*, which is in the process of being published on Amazon, with a more in-depth look and guidelines for a healthy lifestyle, diet, and mindset.

For my clients, such as Shantel, implementing the regimens shared here, added to her personalized recommendations, meant more energy and less anxiety and stress, thereby fulfilling personal and professional goals.

For your personalized and constitutionally correct daily routines, medicinal herbs, and individualized diet and food program, consider having a functional medicine and Ayurvedic consultation.

You may also consider one of my online wellness programs either for yourself or for your employees. I also offer corporate wellness programs to executives and employees. You can find my website here at www.yourvitalitydoctor.com, and you can book a thirty-minute free health and wellness strategy consultation: calendly.com/dr-atousamahdavi/health-strategy-call.

ABOUT ATOUSA MAHDAVI

Dr. Atousa Mahdavi has been practicing holistic medicine for the last twenty-five years in a hands-on clinical setting, working with patients from all walks of life. Her own personal healing journey, along with that of her patients and clients, is a fascinating tale of discovery, learning, and triumphant healing and recovery. A doctor of chiropractic medicine and certified in functional medicine, Ayurvedic medicine, and yoga therapy, she has a unique combination of areas of expertise that make her methods effective in the long term.

She has a deep longing to end human suffering from chronic ailments and is passionate about educating the public that a wellness model of medicine is superior to the current sick-care model of medicine. With a holistic approach and a profound understanding and knowledge of the human system and the mechanics of wellness and health, she has helped many of her patients and clients gain optimal health and well-being. She believes that healing the whole person involves a lifelong commitment to one's well-being, physically, mentally, and spiritually.

She can be reached at dr.atousamahdavi@gmail.com.

CHAPTER 18:

NEVER FAILING FAITH AND HOPE

BY JOYCE LACEY

My mother, June Lynne Lacey, was an amazing woman. She taught me some of life's most important lessons by living an upstanding life. In other words, she truly practiced what she preached.

My mother was no stranger to hardships. Her entire life consisted of one challenge after another. Nonetheless, she always had a positive attitude and a firm faith in God. She trusted Bible Scripture and relied on God's promises to get her through.

When she was born, she was so small that they placed her in a shoebox. She wasn't expected to live, but she surprised everyone! The entire congregation lifted her up in prayer, and her fighting spirit prevailed!

When it came time to deliver me, she asked my father to take her to the doctor, as she wasn't feeling well, but he just took off for the fields to farm. Her water broke and she began bleeding profusely. She crawled to the phone to call her father out of a county board meeting and he rushed us to the hospital. It was a miracle that she could manage to make it to the phone and save our lives. We both would have perished that day.

Because my mother had lost so much blood, she wasn't expected to live. So she was sent home to die in peace. Nonetheless, my mother's fighting spirit and her faith in God sustained her. She was determined to rear her only daughter and stood fast on the promises of God.

Because my father did not want to be burdened with a sickly wife and colicky child who cried constantly, my grandmother took on the task of caring for us both. She was extraordinary! She nursed my mother back to health while dealing with a child with colic.

Unfortunately, my father was hoping for a boy, so he was very disappointed to get a daughter. My mother and he never divorced or legally separated; they just lived apart. My grandparents died when I was very young, so my mother was on her own to rear me.

Although we didn't have many material possessions, we had each other, and the Lord always provided the necessities we needed. We never sought government assistance. I washed dishes in school to help cover the cost of school lunches and later wrote sports stories for the local newspapers, waitressed, worked as a store clerk, and babysat to cover living costs. My mother worked as well.

Unfortunately, some people can be very cruel and judgmental. I remember answering the phone once to have a woman, who thought I was my mother, curse me out for rearing my daughter on my own. Oh, what pure hell my mother endured. Yet she never dreamed of retaliating, though she knew who this woman was. She tried to follow the Ten Commandments and live according to God's Word.

She taught me to turn the other cheek and always do unto others as you would have others do unto you. She taught me to love my neighbor as myself. She was an outstanding example of what I had hoped to become. Her character was exemplary. She was an inspiration to all who knew her.

Because she had given up so much, in order that I could have a wonderful life, I wanted to allow her to experience some joy in her later years. I got her involved in modeling and working on films and television shows. Since she was always volunteering for a worthy cause on a daily basis, I entered her in a seniors' pageant. She won and went on to win three more titles, one in the summer of 2018. She was named National Ms. Super Senior Sweetheart USA at the national pageant in Las Vegas, Nevada!

Naturally, the press did a beautiful story on her. She was in nearly every newspaper statewide, including the statewide seniors' newspaper. She had a four-page write-up in the local magazine, and she was in *Pageantry* and *Good Housekeeping* magazines and on the television news.

Well, it seems that two of the residents in her building became very jealous and disgusted over her fame and decided to start a petition to have her evicted. They sat in the community room gossiping and asked everyone to sign a petition. You see, my mother used oxygen periodically. These bullies told everyone that her oxygen tanks were going to blow up the building! Neither my mother nor I smoked, so that was highly unlikely. Nonetheless, they succeeded in getting her evicted, since one of them was related to a staff member.

After that, I took my mother to the doctor and was met with a very rude nurse. One of the ladies who worked with the wheelchairs overheard this nurse and encouraged me to report her. So I did.

This was a huge mistake. A week later, social services showed up, accusing me of saying that I reused a catheter on my mother. I never reused catheters and showed them all we had in stock. I gave the social worker the name of the company and of my mother's doctor. Since my mother was sleeping, she said she would talk with her later. I called the administration and asked them why they had retaliated. They said they did not, but the nurse I reported had.

Since the social worker could not meet with my mother immediately and since my mother was forced to move, I was expected to drive her 200 miles back to meet with this social worker. Shortly after moving and after helping with the Alzheimer's Walk, my mother said she wasn't feeling well. Because it was the weekend, I took her to the ER. They wanted to put her in the hospital for observation, so I agreed. I wanted what was best for her.

The next day a hospitalist doctor, who had never seen her before, a social worker, hospice nurse, and a chaplain all tried to convince me to dump my mother in a nursing home, put her on hospice, and list her as DNR (do not resuscitate)! Well, I naturally refused, as my mother wanted to live. After this, the rude doctor called me a very poor POA (power of attorney), said he had wasted twenty-seven minutes, and asked if I was her legal guardian. Well, my mother always taught me to tell the truth, so I answered, "No, she doesn't need a guardian, she isn't incompetent." I added, "She wants to live."

After that, he said, "She doesn't know what she wants, she has dementia!" Well, she was never diagnosed with dementia and knew very well what she wanted.

I then attempted to call the social worker to tell her my mother was in the hospital, so I would need to reschedule. She never called me back.

Nothing could prepare me for what happened next. On the day she was to be discharged, I was presented with a paper that stated they had gone over my head and gotten an emergency guardianship/conservatorship to take control of her life! I was told she was to be moved to a nursing home 210 miles from her home, to which my mother commented: "No, I don't want to go to a nursing home!" That was the last thing she said with a clear mind. After that, she was drugged continuously to make her seem incompetent. I asked what drug they were giving her and was told it was morphine. I told them they could not do that and the nurse replied that neither I nor my mother had any say in the matter—as the guardian had instructed them to use any and all means necessary to force my mother to comply.

My mother was forced into a for-profit, fraudulent guardianship, medically kidnapped and trafficked 210 miles from her home to a negligent nursing home, operated by the guardian's company. This was a death sentence ordered in probate court, which is not a court of law, so human rights and U.S. Constitutional Rights are not heard or taken into consideration. She was made a "ward" — in other words, "property" — of the state! She pleaded to go home, but was completely ignored.

I found out a year after my mother died that the attorney I hired should have thrown this case out of that court, as my mother was out of their jurisdiction, but did not because this unscrupulous attorney didn't want to lose her $9,000 retainer fee and was on the board for guardianships and conservatorships. A total conflict of interest!

My mother suffered so that the attorney, nursing home, and guardian could make more money off of her. Isolated in the nursing home, my mother was not allowed outside, not permitted to have a phone, forced to only use a bedpan to go to the bathroom, and constantly drugged, against her will and against her family's wishes. She was tortured before COVID-19, along with who knows how many thousands of others! Guardianships are a very profitable and corrupt business.

After less than three weeks, she came down with pneumonia, a staph infection, septic blood, bumps and bruises, a UTI, bed sores, and a temperature of 102! They had to take her to the hospital, as she was not DNR. She fought all that, with prayer and the will to live, only to be forced back to the same nursing home that nearly killed her!

Although I found a reputable nursing home near the hospital, the guardian forced her to go 80 miles back to their negligent facility, where the nursing home doctor put her on hospice. She was forced to die, with no terminal illness whatsoever.

The oxycodone they forced her to take made it difficult for her to breathe and swallow and caused intense migraine headaches, irregular heartbeat, terrible chest and stomach pain, extreme constipation, and seizures, yet hospice and her guardian insisted she take it. They were even going to take her off all her heart meds and leave her only on the drugs that were killing her, but I pointed out that was murder! I was threatened with arrest if I so much as even took her outside the door!

I called adult protection services four times and got four letters back from social services saying "they decided not to investigate." Even the ombudsman refused to investigate! The local police officer told me that my mother would have more rights if she were a convicted criminal. At least they can refuse being drugged.

The last day, the hospice nurse said her blood pressure was low, so I begged her to get her to the hospital. The hospice nurse refused and she left. My mother stopped breathing, so I called 911. They came out and resuscitated her, but the ER doctor refused to take her in because he said her pulse was too weak, though I pleaded with them to at least try to bring her into the ER. The paramedic, EMT, and everyone just walked away! How could they be so cruel? How do they sleep at night? Don't they take a vow to heal people and not to walk away and let them die?!

Not a day goes by that I don't relive that horror of the torture and hell they put my mother through.

SERVING THE VULNERABLE

With COVID-19, doctors, paramedics, and EMTs continue to decide who lives and dies. For example, Michael Hickson, a forty-six-year-old father and quadriplegic from Texas who'd contracted COVID-19, was taken off treatment in intensive care and placed in hospice. Like my mother, he was heavily medicated and died. Like my mother and I, he and his family did not consent to hospice. He, too, was denied potentially lifesaving treatment because doctors at the hospital made the decision, based on biases, that because of his disabilities, he had a low quality of life.

They use the old, "Oh, you don't want them to suffer, do you?" Well, where are we going to draw the line? Everyone suffers with something. For years, they have used it to convince pregnant women to abort children with Down syndrome or physical defects, when in reality those children were created by God, had a purpose, and may have been the happiest children alive! Only God should make those life-and-death decisions. But it has become the norm now to eliminate the so-called "surplus population," as Scrooge so put it.

I started a nonprofit, the June Lynne Lacey Foundation, in my mother's honor, to try to help others facing this horror. We serve vulnerable adults and children, the elderly, disabled, and our veterans. During the pandemic, we've provided food, necessities, and face masks. We've also arranged drive-by birthday salutes to uplift the spirits of those most isolated by the pandemic and provide scholarships to graduating high school seniors.

As my mother would always say, quoting Scripture: "Fear not, for I am with you." (Is. 41:10) We can always turn to God. He is our strength in times of trouble.

I'm so grateful to have the opportunity to share a little about my mother's challenges in this anthology. As it's been on my heart for many years, I look forward to further revealing the truth to the world by sharing the whole tribulation in my upcoming book, *A True Horror Story of Medical Kidnapping, Fraudulent Guardianship & Death by Hospice.*

We can find comfort in knowing that we are always loved. Our faith can be strengthened and restored, knowing that God holds us in the palm of His hand. "Though I walk through the valley of the shadow of death, I shall fear no evil; for Thou art with me." (Ps. 23:4)

Please remember to get legal guardianship of your loved one(s), as power of attorney does not ensure their wishes are upheld. If they are forced into a fraudulent guardianship, they will suffer a statutory civil death, whereby they henceforth exist only as chattel property (they have no rights).

Please visit and contact us through junelynnelaceyfoundation.com, if you need someone to talk with or know of a vulnerable individual who needs help.

As my mother would always remind me, "Never give up hope! God loves you."

ABOUT JOYCE LACEY

A broadcast journalist, model, actress, teacher, and pastor, Joyce Lacey holds three degrees.

Joyce started out as a sports reporter for the *Grant County Herald* and *Battle Lake Review* and went on to work at KBRF Radio and KBHL Christian Radio. Lacey was named Ms. Minnesota, received a scholarship for Barbizon Modeling School, and went on to model, teach modeling, appear on cable and network television shows, commercials, and in twenty-seven films, including *Beautiful Girls*. She was the executive assistant to the producers of "Let's Bowl" on Comedy Central and had her own talk show on cable.

Lacey has received numerous honors, including being named WCCO Volunteer of the Year, KARE 11 Eleven Who Care recipient, KSTP Everyday Hero, Minnesota State Fair Fifty Year Award, Who's Who Among American Women, the Distinguished American Professionals Award, St. Paul Saints Community Award, and International Women of Distinction Award, just to name a few.

Lacey currently serves as the United States Minnesota Navy League Council's Vice President of Outreach, the Sons of Norway Treasurer, and Chair of the June Lynne Lacey Foundation.

CHAPTER 19:

WALKING BY FAITH

BY CHRISTMAN AND MOLLY HOWARD

What does an old subway receipt have to do with saving a child's life? It's a part of our journey. (More on that later.) Life is quite a journey, isn't it? There are countless possible paths to take. Some are paved with peace, while others are the broken road. Yet no matter the paths taken, we do not travel alone. Entrepreneurship itself is a journey, and we each have a story to tell.

Mark Twain wisely said, "The two most important days in your life are the day you are born and the day you find out why." Maybe it's the discovering of your "why" that has brought you to this book. We believe you were created on purpose, with purpose, and for purpose, and we are excited for you, your journey, and the steps you are taking to change the world.

Perhaps you can pinpoint a person or an occurrence that propelled you onto your entrepreneurial path. Maybe you also have early memories of childhood lemonade stands and bake sales, where young business minds were cultivated. Perhaps you, like us, have learned from previous generations of parents and grandparents who shared their own journeys as entrepreneurs. We each have experiences in life that develop our skills and influence the paths we take.

Several of our family's entrepreneurial adventures followed the knowledge they gained while serving our country during times of war. A television repair shop opened using the skills our grandfather learned as a communications operator in the Navy. Another grandfather implemented his experiences from war to begin a construction company that would build McDonald's restaurants with Ray Kroc. A pair of grandparents applied their knowledge as a nurse and railroad operator to create and secure a patent for a medicinal ointment. We are thankful for our families and the foundations they laid, grounded in faith and the belief that with God, all things are possible.

It takes faith to live in this beautiful yet broken world. It also takes faith to be an entrepreneur. *Harvard Business Review* published an article titled "Entrepreneurs Feel Closer to God Than the Rest of Us Do" by Mitchell J. Neubert. It is based on research investigating "the connection between faith and the propensity to start a business." Neubert reports that perhaps "people with greater faith in God are more willing to take risks. And maybe the individualism and autonomy associated with entrepreneurship are reflected in the idea of a more personal, direct relationship with God."[16]

Similarly, *Entrepreneur* featured the essay "Entrepreneurship Is Not Possible Without Faith." In it, Aniruddha Atul Bhagwat proposes, "It's just not possible to be in control of a situation of uncontrollable elements, and still be confident in your ability to control it without a belief in a power outside of yourself." He continues, "…if you put ten entrepreneurs in a room to discuss miracles in their business; things that happened in the face of failure, which were completely unexpected, one story will follow another, and the stories will be unending."[17] We have experienced this firsthand as God miraculously blessed countless broken roads that led to gracing our family with one of the top independent restaurants in America. Our greatest victories can be just one step beyond our greatest failures. Indeed, triumphs do come through trials and tribulations.

---

16. Mitchell J. Neubert, "Entrepreneurs Feel Closer to God Than the Rest of Us Do," *Harvard Business Review* (October 2013), last accessed January 24, 2021, https://hbr.org/2013/10/entrepreneurs-feel-closer-to-god-than-the-rest-of-us-do.

17. Aniruddha Atul Bhagwat, "Entrepreneurship is Not Possible Without Faith." *Entrepreneur India* (March 30, 2017), last accessed January 24, 2021, https://www.entrepreneur.com/article/292179.

Often in life, there are breakdowns before there are breakthroughs. In 2007–2008, while expecting our first child, we prayed for a project that would be used for God's glory and to bless and encourage others. We were given a dream to create Scripture Socks, where Bible verses are inscribed on the soles of socks, encouraging others to walk by faith and stand on the promises of God. We made homemade versions of Scripture Socks throughout the years, both to give and wear, with hopes to offer comfort from soul to sole. It's surprising how putting on a simple pair of socks can serve as a reminder that our steps in life are filled with God's promise and purpose. In 2017, we felt the quickening of our hearts for Scripture Socks to expand beyond our personal reach. We were working day and night to make the dream a reality, and then the spiritual battle of our lives began.

It's a mystery how life works that way. In one moment, the sun kisses your face as you find shapes in white, fluffy clouds. In the next moment, those same clouds darken and pour the rain, even as your skin is still warm from the sunshine from just seconds before. The blessing is that although the skies may pour, the sun is still there. It never leaves fully. It is only temporarily hidden, waiting to shine again through the darkness.

Perhaps in the darkness our sense of hearing is sharpened. Margaret Feinberg reveals in her book, *The Sacred Echo*, "Often when God speaks, He will say the same thing through a sermon, a passage of Scripture, a chance conversation, or an unexpected encounter. When we begin looking for these sacred echoes, we are better able to recognize God's voice … and walk more confidently in the fullness of what God has for us."[18] We know this to be true.

During church one Sunday morning, in the summer of 2017, our son asked to draw the message that was projected on a screen. We gave him a scrap piece of paper from the inner pocket of his dad's jacket. He wrote, as his grandfather preached, the words of the sermon title, "Knowing and Doing the Will of God." We tucked his drawing into our Bible at the conclusion of the service, not knowing how instrumental it later would be. That afternoon, we were given a vision of what the logo for Scripture Socks should be, using the alliteration of S's to form a path

---

18. Margaret Feinberg, *The Sacred Echo: Hearing God's Voice in Every Area of Your Life* (Grand Rapids, MI: Zondervan, 2008).

to reflect the verse that God's "...Word is a lamp unto my feet and a light unto my path." (Ps. 119:105) We were thrilled to move forward with the vision, trusting we were taking faithful steps in knowing and doing the will of God.

Within weeks, our world turned upside down overnight. Among trials and tests in our attempts to begin the business of Scripture Socks, our daughter became ill with a common virus that caused inflammation of her beautiful brain. The world as our family had known it suddenly changed. We cried out to God in weeps we had not wailed yet. There were so many unknowns during those deeply dark days, but what always was known was that the light of God's presence would overcome the darkness. There is sweetness in surrender. We came to the end of ourselves with the realization that we either trust God or we don't; there is no in-between. Yet we often live in the in-between. We chose to trust Him as we blindly walked by faith.

There were countless ways God made Himself known to us, including messages printed on hospital mattresses and prophetic words from family members and complete strangers in the hospital's halls. Sacred echoes surrounded us, and we found deeper breaths of faith with each one. We inhaled hope and exhaled praise. Through a series of miracles, we received recommendations and faced choosing between two pediatric neurologist specialists: one in North Carolina, less than a four-hour drive from our home, and the other in New Jersey, which was triple the distance. It made sense to choose the closer and more convenient path in this journey, but we fervently prayed for God's guidance.

During one of our innumerable prayers for peace and direction, a piece of paper fell out of our Bible. The sweet drawing of "Knowing and Doing the Will of God" from months before suddenly stared at us. Curious about the unique folds of the little piece of scrap paper that had been taken from the sports coat pocket in church, we turned it over to see which receipt had been used as our son's canvas. The following words greeted us: "NJ Transit: The Way to Go." It was an old subway receipt from a business trip to the northeast four months prior, but in that moment, to us, it was the voice of God.

By God's amazing grace, within twenty-four hours of visiting the specialist in New Jersey, we began seeing miraculous healing in our daughter. She returned to us. In God's infinite wisdom and sovereignty, He had allowed us to go through such unknowns, including our suffering a miscarriage during those same months, so that we could face the choice to walk by faith wholeheartedly, enabling us to be more fully capable of encouraging others to do the same through Scripture Socks. As we love God and are called according to His purpose, we trust that all things work together for our good and His glory. There is purpose in the pain, and the breaking of us can be the making of us. Through the depths of despair, we experienced the heights of God's peace. In the heights of our pain, we felt the depths of His love. We were broken to be made whole.

Although this is but a small portion of our story, we share it with hopes of encouraging you to do the same. As entrepreneurs, we have a calling to share our journeys to help propel others in theirs. In joy and in suffering, there is healing in the telling. The overcoming of our mistakes and losses can encourage others with hope to overcome their own. We each have an opportunity to grow through what we go through in life. Joy C. Brown (who is our mother/mother-in-law) shares in her book *Finding Joy* that many of her life lessons "were learned in the valleys rather than on the mountaintops." "It's all a journey," she writes, and it's a journey worth sharing.[19]

Advanced technology widely opens doors to having your voice be heard. Podcasts, blogs (that can be compiled into books!), and social media platforms are but a few ways to share your story. Yet also in the current world of technology, it's too easy to camouflage truth. With photo filters and perfect poses, authenticity often is masked. We must remember that it's difficult for people to connect with those to whom they cannot relate. We encourage you to be transparent and vulnerable in the sharing of your journey. Life is a beautiful gift that often is quite messy. Others can find healing in the sharing of our deepest hurts, and revealing our scars can help them have hope for the healing of their still-bleeding wounds.

In this way, success is in significance. We each will leave a legacy (for the good or the bad), and we have such a brief time on earth to live the dash between birth and death. How we live will influence who we serve, and true success is not determined by the amount of money we make but by the number of lives we impact for the good. Zig Ziglar taught, "Success is not measured by what you do compared to what others do; it is measured by what you do with the ability God gave you." We each were created uniquely in the very image of God, so that makes us creators too. We are called to be fruitful and productive with the gifts that God gives us.

We each have dreams to awaken and purposes to fulfill. We can stifle them and let the world change us, or we can use them to help change the world. Please never give up on your dreams or your calling. Although the journey at times may be difficult, it's more difficult to regret not taking the first step. Our walks of faith can be wearisome, but they are filled with certain hope, and we each are beckoned to "Live a life worthy of the calling[s] [we] have received." (Eph. 4:1) There is a message for the world, solely yours, that only you can give.

An anonymous soul profoundly wrote, "What we are is God's gift to us, but what we become is our gift to God." We personally pray to be living examples of walking by faith, with our hearts fluent in praise. Our Creator graciously has given each of us the gift of life, filled with

---

19. Joy C. Brown, *Finding Joy: 70 Life Lessons Along the Way* (Maitland, FL: Xulon Press, 2018).

promise and purpose, and the free will to choose the paths we take or pave. In your life's journey, you have a unique footprint that only you can leave on this earth. Although the paths ahead are unknown, we do not need to fear them, for we never walk alone. Listen for sacred echoes. Enjoy the journey. Change the world. One faithful step at a time.

ABOUT CHRISTMAN AND MOLLY HOWARD

Christman and Molly Howard met while in the seventh grade and have been married since 1998. They are blessed with their children Mazi Grace and Bronson, and they reside in Myrtle Beach, SC. Christman serves on the board of the Wall College of Business at Coastal Carolina University, which is the couple's alma mater and where Molly taught. The couple serves in various capacities in numerous businesses and non-profit organizations. Through trials and tribulations, God has graced the Howard family with one of the largest seafood restaurants in America. Christman is a founding member of Metatomic Energy, a company which holds patents for the elimination of nuclear wastes. Christman and Molly pray that their lives will bring glory to God and draw others to Him, and they hope to fulfill their own lives' purposes while encouraging others to do the same. They invite you to join them at www.mollybhoward.com to learn more about Scripture Socks and their family's walks of faith. Please also visit www.businessblueprintguide.com for complimentary resources available to support you in your own entrepreneurial journey.

CHAPTER 20:

COMMUNITY REFORM /
PRISON REFORM / SOCIAL REFORM
(THE NOBILITY OF PEACE IN STRIVING TO BUILD/
REFORM A NOBLE WORLD)

BY BASHIR MUHAMMAD-JORDAN

Bismillah … As-salamu alaykum — may peace/blessing/friendship be upon the readers and the world!

What are some "best practices" in using our influence to change the world? I openly state and testify that he, the Prophet Muhammad (peace and blessing be upon him), is considered the most influential person ever within the history of the world. I encourage you to do your independent research and fact-check. You can start with the simple book *The 100: A Ranking of the Most Influential Persons in History* by Michael H. Hart.

I would like to focus on and introduce five figures who have influenced American social reform as well as world reform. I am *not* going to highlight the noble, exemplary, world-changing character and life works of Prophet Muhammad (peace and blessings be upon him). They will be too extensive to elaborate on and explain within this writing.

"IN THE NAME OF GOD, THE GRACIOUS, THE COMPASSIONATE"

CAN GOD REALLY
CHANGE SOMEONE???

"Allaah (God) Does Not Change The Condition of a Person
Until they Change That Which is in themselves" [13:11]

To whom coming, as unto a living stone,
Disallowed indeed of men, but chosen of God, and Precious
Wherefore also it is contained in the scripture,
Behold, I lay in Zi'on on A chief Corner Stone,
Elect, Precious:
And he that believeth on him shall not be confounded
Unto you therefore which believe he is precious:
But unto them which be disobedient, the stone which
The builders disallowed, the same is made
HEAD OF THE CORNER
Holy Scripture: 1 Peter 2:6

THE BIOGRAPHY/CASE OF
BASHIR MUHAMMAD-JORDAN

Bashir becoming a Certified Dental Assistant and a Certified Dental Technician.
He graduated with excellent to outstanding overall achievement.

A True Short Story of Life
Protected, Transformed and
Changed by the Power of God
Past Gang Member to Present Youth Mentor to Future Oral Surgeon

In all humility and all respect to the people I'm writing about, instead of myself, I'm going to briefly mention five figures who are far less superior than the Prophet Muhammad (peace and blessings be upon him); nevertheless, they were also great world reformers and influencers — and for sure, far more superior than myself.

1. Bilal Ibn Rabah:

The former slave companion, the first person to openly make the call to prayer and summon all of humanity (all colors and races) to bow down in unified/congregational prayer. Bilal rose to prominence in the Islamic community of Madina, as Muhammad (peace and blessing be upon him) appointed him; he became the first treasurer of Islam who was in charge/minister of the Bayt al-Mal (treasury). Islam was becoming and had become the world power. In this capacity, Bilal distributed funds to widows, orphans, wayfarers, and others who could not support themselves.

2. Mansa Musa:

According to Islamic, African, and world historians and a number of sources, Abubakari II, Mansa (king) of the Mali empire in the 14th century, led Malian sailors to the Americas and established trade with the people, along with peace and friendship treaties. This was nearly 200 years before Columbus arrived. Many agree that there was a Black African presence in the Americas way before Columbus. Tiemoko Konate, head of the project tracing Abubakari II's journeys, told the BBC that Columbus himself said he found "Black" traders already present in the Americas.[20] Moreover, chemical analyses of gold tips that Columbus found on spears in America show that the gold probably came from West Africa. Some say that beyond Columbus, evidence of African contributions to American civilization includes "importing the art of pyramid building, political systems and religious practices as well as mathematics, writing and a sophisticated calendar."

His brother Musa was the tenth Mansa of the great Mali empire, an Islamic West African state. He has been described as a great influencer, the wealthiest individual of the Middle Ages and of all of human history. If it were not for him discharging his fifth obligation to Islam, Hajj, the pilgrimage to Mecca, many people would not have known of him. On his pilgrimage to Mecca, going and coming from Hajj, there were documented accounts that he gave away so much charity of gold and

20. Joan Baxter, "Africa's 'greatest explorer," BBC World News, December 13, 2000, http://news.bbc.co.uk/2/hi/africa/1068950.stm.

other valuables and empowering others that he impacted and shifted the entire economy of the world.

3. Muhammad III:

Sultan Muhammad III revived the city of Essaouira and invited Jews and the English to trade there. Merchants from Europe arrived, and the city began to enjoy its golden age. The sultan decided to make it the most important port of the kingdom. He permitted different tribes to inhabit the city and consulates to be established: Denmark first, then France, Brazil, and Portugal. This intelligent and tolerant sultan even welcomed an important Jewish community, which contributed greatly to the development of the city.

Mogador became the first Moroccan port to trade with the non-Islamic world. In 1767, he signed a peace treaty with Spain and a trade agreement with France. Under Mohammed III, Morocco became the first country to recognize the United States as an independent nation, in 1777. The very first president of the United States, George Washington, wrote letters to the sultan in 1789, asking him for aid in allowing American ships to navigate nearby waters and thanking him for help with releasing American sailors captured in Tripoli. It also became the destination for caravans bringing African riches from Timbuktu.

4. El Hajj Malik El Shabazz/Malcolm X:

In the 1960s, Malcolm X began to grow disillusioned with the Nation of Islam, as well as with its leader Elijah Muhammad. He subsequently embraced Sunni Islam (as practiced by the Prophet Muhammad, peace and blessings be upon him) and the civil rights movement after completing the Hajj to Mecca, and became known as El-Hajj Malik El-Shabazz. After a brief period of travel across Africa, he publicly renounced the Nation of Islam and founded the Islamic Muslim Mosque, Inc. (MMI) and the Pan-African Organization of Afro-American Unity (OAAU).

Malcolm wrote a famous letter from Mecca, "The Pilgrimage to Mecca." On April 13, 1964, Malcolm X left the United States on a personal and spiritual journey through the Middle East and West Africa.

By the time he returned on May 21, he had visited Egypt, Lebanon, Saudi Arabia, Nigeria, Ghana, Morocco, and Algeria. When he was in Mecca, El-Hajj Malik El-Shabazz wrote a letter to his loyal assistants in Harlem from his heart:

> "Never have I witnessed such sincere hospitality and overwhelming spirit of true brotherhood as is practiced by people of all colors and races here in this ancient Holy Land, the home of Abraham, Muhammad and all the other Prophets of the Holy Scriptures. For the past week, I have been utterly speechless and spellbound by the graciousness I see displayed all around me by people of all colors.
>
> "I have been blessed to visit the Holy City of Mecca, I have made my seven circuits around the Ka'ba, led by a young Mutawaf named Muhammad, I drank water from the well of the Zam Zam. I ran seven times back and forth between the hills of Mt. Al-Safa and Al Marwah. I have prayed in the ancient city of Mina, and I have prayed on Mt. Arafat.
>
> "There were tens of thousands of pilgrims, from all over the world. They were of all colors, from blue-eyed blondes to black-skinned Africans. But we were all participating in the same ritual, displaying a spirit of unity and brotherhood that my experiences in America had led me to believe never could exist between the white and non-white.
>
> "America needs to understand Islam, because this is the one religion that erases from its society the race problem. Throughout my travels in the Muslim world, I have met, talked to, and even eaten with people who in America would have been considered white — but the white attitude was removed from their minds by the religion of Islam. I have never before seen sincere and true brotherhood practiced by all colors together, irrespective of their color.

"You may be shocked by these words coming from me. But on this pilgrimage, what I have seen, and experienced, has forced me to rearrange much of my thought-patterns previously held, and to toss aside some of my previous conclusions. This was not too difficult for me. Despite my firm convictions, I have always been a man who tries to face facts, and to accept the reality of life as new experience and new knowledge unfolds it. I have always kept an open mind, which is necessary to the flexibility that must go hand in hand with every form of intelligent search for truth."

From *The Autobiography of Malcolm X*
Taken from http://islam.uga.edu/malcomx.html

5. Muhammad Ali:

Muhammad Ali was an American professional boxer, activist, and philanthropist. Nicknamed "the Greatest," he is widely regarded as one of the most significant and celebrated figures of the 20th century and as the greatest boxer, athlete, and professional sports figure of all time. In 1966, Ali refused to be drafted into the military, citing his religious beliefs and ethical opposition to the Vietnam War. He was found guilty of draft evasion, so he faced five years in prison and was stripped of his boxing titles. He stayed out of prison as he appealed the decision to the Supreme Court, which overturned his conviction in 1971, but he had not fought for nearly four years and lost a period of peak performance as an athlete.

Ali's actions as a conscientious objector to the Vietnam War made him an icon for the larger counterculture generation, and he was a very high-profile figure of racial pride for African Americans during the civil rights movement and throughout his career. As a Muslim, Ali was initially affiliated with Elijah Muhammad's Nation of Islam (NOI). He later disavowed the NOI, adhering to Sunni Islam (as practiced by the Prophet Muhammad, peace and blessings be upon him) and supporting Islamic racial integration like his former mentor Malcolm X.

We are appealing to world leaders! Our target audience is the caring, compassionate, and noble families of royalty, the ultra-wealthy, truly affluent entrepreneurs/corporations, and the truly philanthropic people of the world to help those who are really in need! I have a team that is certified/qualified/bona fide to bring about a cure, and we are willing/ready/able to do the work which requires resources, finances, and your support.

We have been and are here in the worst of prisons, communities, hoods, trenches, and grassroots, giving the people the best of us as opposed to the worst of us, on a mission working/aiming to get inner city youth, alleged organizational/gang members, tribal leaders/followers, Muslims, Christians, Jews, and others to select sharing/caring over selfishness and being uncharitable, peace over war, and nobility over ignobility. Essentially, we are continuing to build our team, our campaign, and our organization, one to ten strong, one to ten solid, and one to ten caring individual(s) at a time.

We are asking everyone we know, as well as asking/recruiting those we do not know, to become involved with our organization at some type of level, according to your means/abilities, and to make two pledges: a giving pledge and a peace pledge. The work we have done, are doing and, Creator willing, will continue to do, I/we bear witness, I/we are an example and I/we are a proof. It truly reforms — it helps solve some of the most pressing problems of America: poverty, crime, depression, suicide, hunger, homelessness, joblessness, racism, inequality, and injustices. It helps people from spending some or all of their lives in prison, falling victim to despair, addictions, violence, and so on. It helps save lives!

President Joe Biden, on his road to achieving such a prominent position of world leadership, quoted a statement attributed to the Prophet Muhammad (peace and blessings be upon him) as saying, "When you see a wrong, you change it with your hand, if not, then with your tongue, and then if not, you hate it within your heart, which is the weakest of faith." When we as world leaders recognize the need to truly establish an egalitarian society, when we acknowledge our wrongs or the wrongs of our forebears and are willing to offer reparations to the wronged, when we have the courage to command the right and forbid the wrong, when we dare to challenge, correct, and change laws and systems that have historically and currently criminalized (enslaved/imprisoned) a certain group of our citizens, when we welcome the responsibility to help guide and mentor our youth, providing and assuring them with "Bright Smile/Bright Futures," when we prioritize the agenda to improve the conditions of the worst cities and communities, elevating them from destruction to production/construction within our country, which is the essence of community reform/prison reform/social reform, and when we use our entrepreneurial abilities, finances, resources, skillsets, and dynamic personalities/positive mental attitude/pure hearts to pursue the nobility of peace as the method, in striving to build a noble world ... We then would have followed in the footsteps of a few of the honorable, dignified, noble people of purpose mentioned within this writing, and then, like them, we would have completed our mission of revolutionizing/changing/influencing the world! Please see the extended version of this writing at Queensteam.org and Mmacinc.org.

ABOUT BASHIR MUHAMMAD-JORDAN

Who is he? Bashir Muhammad-Jordan (aka Dr. Shajeem) is a studying/aspiring oral surgeon and student of sacred knowledge, an author, speaker, father, philanthropist, consultant, and chairman of the nonprofit Queens Team Motivational/Inspirational Community Organization (Queens Team Edu'Tainment/Queens Team Reform Alliance-NewYork2Atlanta) and Team Muslim Enterprises. He's a member of the International Documentary Association and a member of Team Clean (a purification firm of dedicated individuals who are OSHA 500&30-certified, Serve Safe-certified, Universal Precaution-certified and Health Dept., EPA, and CDC-informed, studying/developing best practices and safe/ natural ways to effectively clean your home/business, preserve your health, produce oxygen, improve indoor air quality, etc., who have joined the fight to eliminate/reduce the spread of COVID-19 and save lives). He's a founder, collaborating partner and/or is associated with the Aboriginal American Ahlus Sunnah Wa Jama'ah Nation of Islam (ANOI), Black Imams Roundtable, SAVE Institute/Inner City Muslim Action Network, Muslim Alliance of North America, Islamic Young Men's Movement, Malcolm X Grassroots Movement, Black Man's Lab (Consequences of Thug Life/Let Us Make Man), From Destruction2Production, From Prison To Purpose Org./ From Prison To Power Org., Great Southern Jordan Ranch & Family Farm(s)/Mr. Everything (Halal), Grow Up-Grow Out Org. and North/South-East Coast: Credible Messengers.

Bashir's earnest desire, in the words of one of our Black Man's Lab organizational members and a "Link In Our Chain and It Won't Break Here," Mr. Keith Lewis Jr., is to be a "father first," a leader of positive example to his eldest son as well as a continued guiding and loving father to his youngest sons, grandchildren, and all children within our communities of America and internationally, empowering them with "Bright Smiles/Bright Futures" on their journey of purpose as they prudently avoid the "rocky roads" of bad decision-making within our noble world! Along with this anthology, by Best Seller Publishing and our ultra-talented group of authors, co-writers, colleagues, and entrepreneurs, Bashir is working on a collective cultural series/book study project, in a soon-to-be-released book/ podcast/docu-series/movie series called *Letters To Our Sons*. Bashir believes *Letters To Our Sons*, from a doctoral-level dissertation, social work health study, and conflict resolution perspective, will have a greater positive community/prison/social reform impact than any project he has worked on from 1980 to 2020–21, as of to date, dealing with this subject matter.